DEPRESSION
MATTERS

DEPRESSION
MATTERS

Dr Susan Musikanth

DELTA BOOKS · JOHANNESBURG

All rights reserved.
No part of this publication may be reproduced
or transmitted, in any form or by any means,
without prior permission from the publisher.

© Dr Susan Musikanth 1997

Published in 1997 by
Delta Books
A DIVISION OF JONATHAN BALL PUBLISHERS (PTY) LTD
P O Box 33977
Jeppestown 2043

ISBN 0 908387 80 6

Names and circumstances of clients discussed in this book have been changed to protect their identities and respect their privacy. Depression is an illness that frequently needs professional diagnosis and treatment. While this book sets out to offer practical self-help it must be stressed that if the depression is severe and/or persists after working through this book a psychiatrist or psychologist should be consulted.

Design by Michael Barnett, Johannesburg
Typesetting and reproduction of cover by RT Sparhams (Pty) Ltd, Johannesburg
Typesetting and reproduction of text by Book Productions, Pretoria
Printed by National Book Printers, Drukkery Street, Goodwood, Western Cape

CONTENTS

INTRODUCTION	1
PART 1	
DESCRIPTION OF DEPRESSION	7
How do you and I describe depression?	7
If you are a depressed person how do you experience depression?	7
What is it like for you to be closely associated with a depressed person?	27
The therapist's description of depression	39
Summary	47
PART 2	
SELF-HELP AND DEPRESSION	51
Exercise	52
Deep muscle relaxation with creative visualisation and music	56
Saying No – 'gut'-stuff	62
Creativity	66
Religious/spiritual support	69
Positive thinking	72
Touch – sensual and sexual	75
Space	78
Humour	80
Nutrition	81

Financial management	84
Summary	87

PART 3

MEDICAL APPROACH TO AND TREATMENT OF DEPRESSION	91
Psychotropic medication	94
Electroshock therapy	104
Summary	107

PART 4

PSYCHOTHERAPY WITH DEPRESSION	111
What are some of the psychological theories and therapies used in treatment of depression?	111
Summary	131

PART 5

HOLISTIC APPROACH TO DEPRESSION	135
Acupuncture	137
Alexander Technique	138
Aromatherapy	138
Homoeopathy	139
Reflexology	142
Summary	143

CONCLUDING COMMENTS	144
FOOTNOTES	145
RECOMMENDED READING	149

*This book is dedicated to my sons,
Evan and Paul Musikanth
with love.*

ACKNOWLEDGEMENTS
My sincere thanks to:

My clients and delegates for sharing their lives with me and for our mutual learning.
Adele Rifkin for typing and correcting the manuscript, over and over and often into the early hours of the morning.
Kerry Abramowitz for shaping and sharpening the manuscript and for her delightful sense of humour.
My publishers, Jonathan Ball, for understanding the project and undertaking to publish.
Gregory Abramowitz for invaluable help with computer gremlins.
Dr Nathan Finkelstein for generous advice on and checking of the psychotropic medication information contained in this book.
Joe Talmud for his help with information about the classification and side-effects of antidepressants.
Doryce Sher for invaluable input on the benefits of aromatherapy with depression.
Felicity Fine for her expert advice on homoeopathy with depression.
The management and staff of Piazza Trevi, Nando's Tokai and Robbins Coffee Shop for their hospitality and support through the months that I was writing this book.
My friend and colleague, Irene Berman for bearing with me through this book and for offering incisive and insightful suggestions.
Dr Connie Valkin for friendship and creative input from a respected psychotherapist's perspective.
Sharon Kaufmann for her exquisite empathic guidance throughout.
Dorothy Kowen for her way with words and for her integrity.
Neville Serman for consistent practical and emotional support and large doses of humour through this difficult subject.

INTRODUCTION

It was New Year's Day. Rob, 39, had been admitted to hospital. His girlfriend, Sara, 27, was sitting on his bed, holding his hand. I introduced myself and explained that their doctor had asked me to come and talk to Rob.

Rob complained that he had been feeling terrible. He had been suffering from stomach cramps and headaches. He had been feeling so tired that he could hardly get out of bed. His muscles and bones ached. 'I feel like such a failure – I just cannot cope.' He told me that he had been given a promotion two weeks earlier, and was now General Manager of his company. From the time of his promotion Rob had felt himself becoming more and more depressed.

He described himself as a perfectionist who hated change and who, from time to time, became highly stressed. When this happened he struggled to sleep at night, and had hardly any appetite.

Now too, he said, 'I don't feel like eating and, while I do fall asleep at 12 or 1 a.m., I can't sleep deeply. I always wake again at 3 or 4 a.m. Then I just walk around. I feel so bad, I've let so many people down.' He looked at Sara. 'She has really been there for me. I don't deserve her.'

Then Rob started to sob. Sara put her arms around him and held him until he quietened. He spoke almost in a whisper, 'My father would have been so disappointed to see me like this. He died five years ago, and he knew that I was strong and could cope. I tried to help him through his illness. I nursed him and fed him with a spoon when he couldn't feed himself. I even protected my mother and sisters from the fact that Dad was going to die. I couldn't save him.' Then Rob cried for a long time.

I asked Sara how she saw the problem, and how she was managing. She admitted to me that she wanted to get married but that Rob was frightened of commitment. She had met Rob at work where she had been hired as his secretary. She said, 'I was a heavy-drinking social animal. Rob was so solid, so kind and quiet – I knew that he was right for me. I knew that he liked me, but he wasn't making any moves so one day I attacked him in his office, and kissed him on his mouth.' Sara and Rob smiled at the memory. She told me that Rob, although a perfectionist, coped exceptionally well at work. 'Head Office sees him as the "Golden Boy" and has promoted him faster than any other employee. He works so hard and comes home very late at night.'

Then Sara admitted to me, 'He does everything for his Mom. Sometimes I feel that he gives her more attention than he gives me. Ever since I have known him, Rob has eaten very poorly, and hardly slept at all at night.

'He comes home from work, switches on the television and that's him for the night. We hardly ever have sex. The worst thing is that we never go on holiday together. He doesn't mind if I go away with my parents, but I wish that he would come too.

'I think that Rob has been depressed since his father died, many many years ago. It is showing at work now. I love him very much, and I try hard to get him to go out for a meal or to exercise. I wish that he would stop being such a perfectionist. Everything he does has to be absolutely flawless. He will not allow himself to make a single slip or error.'

I listened to Rob and Sara telling their story. I noted the tones of their voices and watched their body-language. I asked questions about their families, and the patterns of behaviour that had been seen as normal when the couple had been growing up. Most importantly, I wanted to know how Rob and Sara, their respective families and possibly their work systems were operating to keep Rob depressed.

It was our first session, but already I could see that Rob was severely depressed: his skin colour was greyish-yellow. His voice was monotonous and he spoke slowly. His eyes were dull. He held his head in his hands. His mouth seemed to turn down, and he cried easily. He spoke negatively about himself. He looked fearful and highly anxious. Sara, too, looked depressed, but her focus was more on Rob's problem and on trying to 'fix it', than on her own struggle. She had taken on the role of 'caretaker', and was using so much emotional energy that she was becoming exhausted. Sara's mother had rejected her from an early age. She felt that Rob needed her – hence her need to be needed.

Rob's family depended on him an enormous amount. He never imagined saying 'no' to his mother's or sisters' unreasonable demands. Rob had not been able to save his father's life and felt terribly guilty. He now tried to 'make it up' to his mother and sisters by satisfying their every need – to the detriment of his own and Sara's needs. His one area of success had, until now, been at work, but this too was failing.

I thought that perhaps Rob had been promoted in the wrong direction, too fast, or too often, for a person who hated change. These hypotheses would need to be tested in later sessions. Sara ate and slept well, and she exercised on a regular basis. She was fulfilling some of her own needs.

As a therapist, it is important for me to listen to the stories of my depressed clients and those people who are close to them. I need to ask a lot of questions about their present and their past, as I try to find patterns that will make some sense of their problem. I watch carefully for non-verbal body language, and the interactions between the people concerned. I try, in therapy, to include as many members of the depressed system as possible, to maximise the potential for change. Besides working with the client to resolve some of the conflicts and relieve some of the symptoms, I work on my client's close relationships. At times I consult some of the family members and people from work – all with my client's consent. I am at present working with Rob, with Sara, with Rob and Sara together, and with Rob and his superior at his company's head office.

There are many reasons why I am writing this book. The story of Rob and Sara is just one.

It is clear from my research and experience, as well as that of others, that depression is as common as the cold virus. Less information is available, however, about the fact that depression is highly contagious to those close to a depressed person (the spouse, partner, child, parent, sibling, business partner, employer or employee). The reason for writing another book dealing with the subject of depression is to acknowledge the struggle of both the depressed person and those close to him or her. This inclusive approach will, hopefully, offer a measure of relief to all concerned. Further to this, there is an important need for a positive, broad-based repertoire of ways in which to manage depression – whether you are depressed, or are close to a depressed person. To this end, *Depression Matters* includes:

- *Self-help:* exercise, relaxation, creativity, positive thinking and more;
- *The medical approach:* psychotropic medication and electroshock therapy;
- *Psychotherapy:* a synopsis of some of the available psychotherapies, with an illustrative case study
- *The holistic view:* acupuncture, aromatherapy, homoeopathy and more.

I also hold the fervent hope that my relationship with you throughout this book will be a catalyst for your continued conversation with others. In this way we are going to stretch the existing boundaries of knowledge and management of depression.

If you have chosen to read this book because you, or someone close to you, is or has been depressed you are going to derive the most benefit if you work through the process and management of depression with me in a practical and creative manner. To do so, please have the following materials on hand:

- notebook and pen
- tape recorder and a few blank cassettes
- small piece of modelling clay/plasticine
- coloured pencils or felt-tipped pens
- glue
- scissors
- old magazines
- large sheet of blank paper
- a selection of your favourite music

PART 1

DESCRIPTION OF DEPRESSION

HOW DO YOU AND I DESCRIBE DEPRESSION?

We are going to examine depression using creative, practical and informational means, in order that:

- you, the depressed person, will be able to describe how it feels to be depressed.
- you, the person close to someone who is depressed, will be able to examine your difficulties and needs in respect of this situation.
- I, the therapist, can offer information and discussion on how I describe the depressed client and those close to him or her.

IF YOU ARE THE DEPRESSED PERSON, HOW DO YOU EXPERIENCE DEPRESSION?

CLAY MODELLING

Take a piece of modelling clay/plasticine. Roll it into a ball. Switch on your favourite music. Take a few slow, deep breaths and start to mould the clay. Get in touch with the music, and experience how you are feeling in terms of depression, and how you would like to feel in the future.

Let it happen, don't try to accomplish anything. Take your time, and let yourself relax. Model the clay while you listen to the music. You may keep your eyes open or closed. When you have finished, look at your model.

- It may be a person (you)
- It may be a box (controlled)
- It may be a ball (a wish to be whole)
- It may be stretched to breaking point – or it may be none of the above, and something totally different

Examine your model and either explain its significance to someone who is with you, or record it using your tape recorder, or write it on a page of your notebook. By using clay modelling, you are accessing thoughts and feelings deep in your subconscious mind, and bringing them to your conscious mind.

STORYTELLING

Turn to a blank page of your notebook and write your story. If you are right-handed, write with your left hand and vice versa. This taps into your subconscious mind. You may prefer to tell it to someone else, or record it using a tape recorder.

Start with the information that you have learned from your clay model (how you feel at present). Then, go back to the first time you remember feeling depressed. Try to recall the circumstances surrounding you at that time.

You will find that you remember feelings and circumstances that surrounded you at that time. Continue with your story until the present.

At this point, describe your parents, their relationships with each other, and with you and your siblings, if you have any. Try to remember if any member of your family suffered from depression and stress.

If you have information about your grandparents, uncles, aunts and cousins, write about them, too, and see if any of them do – or have previously – struggled with depression. If your parents are still alive, ask them about their parents and grandparents, and others in the family – their general anecdotes about them as well as any patterns of depression. Include these accounts in your story. If your parents are no longer alive, or won't speak or can't remember, ask sisters, brothers, uncles, aunts or possibly neighbours.

The process of storytelling, as with the clay modelling, is a creative way to release some of the heaviness and pain that is inside you. Also, as you write or tell your story, you are remembering episodes in your life and finding out more about your history. Because you have brought to the fore a great deal about yourself in a creative manner, you are likely to feel tired – as if you had run a marathon – but should not feel as heavy or stressed as you felt before you started. While you probably feel some relief, you may be experiencing some vulnerability and even some sadness at what you have learned about yourself.

Take a break now and do something kind for yourself. Depressed people do not usually know how to be kind to themselves. Do for yourself now whatever you would suggest or do for your best friend or your child if they were suffering from depression. Perhaps you will choose to go for a long gentle walk, listen to some soothing music, ask someone close to you to give you a back rub, get into the calming surroundings of nature, or anything that feels nuturing and healing to you.

If you are the person close to someone who is depressed, turn to a blank sheet of paper and try to put yourself in the position of that person. Try to feel how he or she feels, physically and emotionally. Make a heading:

Physical symptoms of depression
Jot down a list of physical symptoms that you think a depressed person experiences, for example, 'headaches'. Turn to a new page and make a heading:

Emotional symptoms of depression
Write a list of the emotional symptoms that you associate with the depressed person you know, for example, 'despair'. Below is the story of my client, Jenny, who was depressed. This will be followed by a questionnaire and a list of some of the physical and emotional symptoms experienced by depressed people.

THE STORY OF JENNY

Jenny, 35, was a divorcee who had no children. She told me that she was at her wits' end because her mother, an alcoholic, was constantly getting drunk and Jenny felt obligated to sort her out and stop her drinking. Jenny said, 'I am so tired, but when I go to bed I cannot sleep. I have lost my appetite and I have no motivation for work. I sometimes think that life has no meaning.'

Her father, also an alcoholic, had been murdered a year before our meeting. She had been married for a short while to a man who drank heavily and physically and emotionally abused her. She had had a satisfying relationship after her marriage with a man she had loved very much. 'I believed that John and I would be happy for ever and build a healthy family together. When John met my family, however, he made an excuse to break off our relationship.' Jenny explained that she had always been strong for her parents, for her younger brother and for her husband. 'I can't understand why I feel so weak now – I can't cope any more.'

'When I think back to my childhood, I can remember coping well with almost anything. Some things were difficult and upsetting and scary but manageable. I remember when I was five or six years old, my parents went to a party. They often went out to parties or movies. I stayed home alone. I was brave. At about the same time, my mom had a hairdressing salon. I used to help her by making her breakfast at the back of the salon. I had to stand on a chair to reach the stove. I also answered the telephone when the salon was busy and would say "Sally's Beauty Salon – good morning." Those are happy memories. My mom was so proud of me and I knew that I was coping well. I also remember visiting my Gran. She made pancakes and flapjacks with lots of syrup and she taught me to crochet. Things got bad though. Weekends were big family get-togethers. We would visit my uncle. Other aunts, uncles and cousins would be there too. We children would run off and play while the grown-ups drank a lot. There were always arguments – we got used to them. They had screaming matches and punch-ups. We children would cry and plead with them to stop. The journey home was usually a nightmare. I would dread it because my father drove so fast when he was drunk. I would duck down on the floor behind the front seat and pray that we would get home safely. I would beg him to slow down – he never listened to me.

'We often went on picnics in a big family group and there, too, everyone would be drinking and raising their voices. I thought alcohol was a terrible thing. It caused so much trouble. I cursed it. I couldn't understand why they drank this stuff that made their personalities change and become aggressive and unbearable. They never looked as if they enjoyed it anyway, because they would down a glass in one gulp and pull the most awful faces. Now I can only think it was for the effect – to escape reality. Often the hangovers from a Sunday session continued into Monday and sometimes Tuesday. They called it "the hair of the dog".

'My dad had a laid-back temperament, but when he was drinking his temper got very bad. He not only had punch-ups with my uncles but he and my mom had bad fights. I used to beg her not to answer back.

'Sometimes I held my hand over her mouth to keep her quiet. He was like a crazy man. She would push me away and continue nagging and cursing him. He would break things and slam doors or hit my mother. She sometimes had black eyes and bruises and bumps. I would get ice packs and put them on her and try to console her. When I was in bed, I could still hear them fighting. When the pitch of their voices grew higher and louder, it was time for me to go and stop them – I tried but it never helped. At times it was really bad. My dad would take out his gun and threaten to shoot my mother. I would scream hysterically and try to get the gun from him.

'My mother was such a flirt with other men – this often caused their fights. Once I found her in bed with a strange man at someone's house. I begged her to come into the lounge where the other people were. After my parents had had a terribly violent fight they would often not talk to each other for days or weeks. That in itself was hell for me. I had to convey messages at mealtimes and they would sleep in separate rooms and barely speak to me. It drove me insane. I would sit at school all day wondering how I could get them to make friends and talk again. The worst of all was that I couldn't bring friends home because I was so ashamed of my parents' behaviour. I want something better for myself. The years that followed were up and down. The drinking periods came and went. Slowly the bingeing periods got longer, and the dry times in between got shorter. I got married against my parents wishes. I went ahead and did it anyway. It turned very sour. I felt so lonely. I knew I could never go to them for help or support. I turned to friends, so they never really knew what was happening in my life. My husband kept on accusing me of putting my parents before him.

'After my divorce, my parents drank more than before. I felt that they were drinking so much because I had let them down. I was available whenever they went on a binge. I no longer lived with them, but I would always go and straighten things out when they got ill. I always seemed to be taking them to hospital or to those rehabilitation homes. It never worked for long. It was like a recurring bad dream. I felt upset because they would be weak from not eating. I would cry and pray and plead with them to look at what they were doing to themselves. I withdrew emotionally from them until all I was, was a body – doing what I had to do as a responsible daughter. I stopped pleading and begging, and tried to shut it out of my thoughts as much as possible. It's so difficult to exclude yourself from the terrible nightmare. A strong sense of duty keeps you hanging in. And then my dad was murdered... Why couldn't my mom just leave him alone and keep quiet? He would still have been alive if she had just listened to me.

'I am in a new town now, slowly feeling less guilty and responsible. I'm accepting that I can no longer be of help. I've built some wonderful friendships, and I would love someone to take care of me. I know I have lots of love to give...'

The story of Jenny will continue later in this book. At this point it would be helpful for you, the depressed client, to complete the following depression inventory to determine your level of depression.

DEPRESSION INVENTORY

Read the statements in each of the categories (A – U) and select the statement that fits you best at the present time. Circle the number next to each statement that you have chosen.

Adapted from Beck, Ward, Mendelson, Mock & Erbach – *An Inventory for Measuring Depression.*

A *(Mood)*
0   I do not feel sad.
1   I feel blue or sad.
2a I feel blue or sad all the time and I can't snap out of it.
2b I am so sad or unhappy that it is very painful.
3   I am so sad or unhappy that I can't stand it.

B *(Pessimism)*
0   I am not particularly pessimistic or discouraged about the future.

1   I feel discouraged about the future.
2a I feel I have nothing to look forward to.
2b I feel that I won't ever get over my troubles.
3   I feel that the future is hopeless and that things cannot improve.

C *(Sense of failure)*
0   I do not feel like a failure.
1   I feel I have failed more than the average person.
2a I feel that I have accomplished very little that is worthwhile or that means anything.
2b As I look back on my life all I can see is a lot of failures.
3   I feel I am a complete failure as a person (parent, husband, wife).

D *(Lack of satisfaction)*
0   I am not particularly dissatisfied.
1a I feel bored most of the time.
1b I don't enjoy things the way I used to.
2   I don't get satisfaction out of anything any more.
3   I am dissatisfied with everything.

E *(Guilty feeling)*
0   I don't feel particularly guilty.
1   I feel bad or unworthy a good part of the time.
2a I feel quite guilty.
2b I feel bad or unworthy practically all the time now.
3   I feel as though I am very bad or worthless.

F *(Sense of punishment)*
0   I don't feel I am being punished.
1   I have a feeling that something bad may happen to me.
2   I feel I am being punished or will be punished.
3a I feel I deserve to be punished.
3b I want to be punished.

G *(Self-hate)*
0   I don't feel disappointed in myself.
1a I am disappointed in myself.
1b I don't like myself.
2   I am disgusted with myself.
3   I hate myself.

H (Self-accusations)
0   I don't feel I am any worse than anybody else.
1   I am very critical of myself for my weaknesses or mistakes.
2a I blame myself for everything that goes wrong.
2b I feel I have many bad faults.

I (Self-punitive wishes)
0   I don't have any thoughts of harming myself.
1   I have thoughts of harming myself but I would not carry them out.
2a I feel I would be better off dead.
2b I have definite plans about commiting suicide.
2c I feel my family would be better off if I were dead.
3   I would kill myself if I could.

J (Crying spells)
0   I don't cry any more than usual.
1   I cry more now than I used to.
2   I cry all the time now. I can't stop it.
3   I used to be able to cry but now I can't cry at all even though I want to.

K (Irritability)
0   I am no more irritated now than I ever am.
1   I get annoyed or irritated more easily than I used to.
2   I feel irritated all the time.
3   I don't get irritated at all at the things that used to irritate me.

L (Social withdrawal)
0   I have not lost interest in other people.
1   I am less interested in other people now than I used to be.
2   I have lost most of my interest in other people and have little feeling for them.
3   I have lost all my interest in other people and don't care about them at all.

M (Indecisiveness)
0   I make decisions about as well as ever.
1   I am less sure of myself now and try to put off making decisions.

2 I can't make decisions any more without help.
3 I can't make any decisions at all any more.

N (Body image)
0 I don't feel I look any worse than I used to.
1 I am worried that I am looking old or unattractive.
2 I feel that there are permanent changes in my appearance and they make me look unattractive.
3 I feel that I am ugly or repulsive-looking.

O (Work inhibition)
0 I can work as well as before.
1a It takes extra effort to get started at doing something.
1b I don't work as well as I used to.
2 I have to push myself very hard to do anything.
3 I can't do any work at all.

P (Sleep disturbance)
0 I can sleep as well as usual.
1 I wake up more tired in the morning than I used to.
2 I wake up 1 – 2 hours earlier than usual and find it hard to get back to sleep.
3 I wake up early every day and can't get more than 5 hours' sleep.

Q (Fatigability)
0 I don't get any more tired than usual.
1 I get tired more easily than I used to.
2 I get tired from doing anything.
3 I get too tired to do anything.

R (Loss of appetite)
0 My appetite is no worse than usual.
1 My appetite is not as good as it used to be.
2 My appetite is much worse now.
3 I have no appetite at all any more.

S (Weight loss)
0 I haven't lost much weight, if any, lately.
1 I have lost more than 2 kilograms.

2   I have lost more than 5 kilograms.
3   I have lost more than 7 kilograms.

T (Somatic preoccupation)
0   I am no more concerned about my health than usual.
1   I am concerned about aches and pains or an upset stomach or constipation or other unpleasant feelings in my body.
2   I am so concerned with how I feel or what I feel that it's hard to think of much else.
3   I am completely absorbed in what I feel.

U (Loss of libido)
0   I have not noticed any recent change in my interest in sex.
1   I am less interested in sex than I used to be.
2   I am much less interested in sex now.
3   I have lost interest in sex completely.

Scoring
Add together the numbers that you have circled. Your total score will indicate your depth of depression:

None	0 – 9
Mild	10 – 18
Moderate	19 – 25
Moderate to severe	26 – 35
Severe	36+

PHYSICAL AND EMOTIONAL SYMPTOMS OF DEPRESSION

This list includes the most common symptoms reported by depressed clients.

Physical Symptoms	*Emotional Symptoms*
Stomach aches	Lack of motivation
Headaches	Negative thoughts
Dizziness	about self,
Heart palpitations	surroundings and the
Muscular pains	future
Fatigue	Poor self-esteem
Poor appetite	Guilt

Poor sleeping habits
Tingling in hands and/or feet
Constipation/diarrhoea
Nausea
Not feeling physically well
Retardation (slow-down at a physical level)

Dependence
Despondence
Hopelessness
Helplessness
Poor concentration
Poor memory
Self-blame
Anxiety
Inassertiveness
Feeling of inadequacy
Feeling of worthlessness
Moodiness
Mood swings
Irritability
Inability to cope
Unhappiness
Boredom
Disinterest
Lack of enjoyment
Psychological retardation (slow-down at an emotional level)
Suicidal thoughts and/or attempts at suicide
Obsessive behaviour
Loss of confidence

TYPES AND CAUSES OF DEPRESSION

Depression has been categorised into various types. These include the following:

- *Reactive, exogenous or neurotic depression* – due to stress, loss, disappointment or other external causes.
- *Endogenous or psychotic depression* – due to unknown (iatrogenic) factors, with the possibility of genetic/biological causes.
- *Major depression* – a disabling depression that interferes with the client's ability to eat, sleep, work or enjoy normal once-pleasurable activities.
- *Dysthymia* – less severe than a major depression, but nevertheless involving long-term, chronic symptoms of

depression, where the client constantly feels fatigued and 'down'. When a client with dysthymia experiences a major depression, it is experienced as doubly severe.
- *Seasonal affective disorder (SAD)* – due to cold, dark climates and recurs every winter.
- *Bereavement* – due to the loss of a loved-one may continue beyond the period regarded as culturally normal. It may thereafter resemble a major depression.
- *Atypical depression* – where the client eats and sleeps more than usual and is able to enjoy certain activities, once he or she is faced with these.
- *Manic-depressive psychosis or bipolar disorder* – alternating and recurring episodes of elation and depression.
- *Post-partum depression* – due to hormonal disturbances which occur after childbirth. This should not be confused with the 'blues' or mild moodiness soon after the birth of a baby.
- *Premenstrual depression and tension* – due to hormonal imbalance which occurs a few days or a few weeks before and sometimes during menstruation.
- *Involutional melancholia* – due to hormonal disturbances which arise with menopause.

The problem with endogenous depression is that no research has proved an exclusively biological (inherited) base for depression. We do know, however, that depression sometimes exists when there is a complete, or relative depletion of certain chemicals or neurotransmitters between the nerve endings in the brain. These chemicals include certain catecholamines. This research has been called 'the catecholamine hypothesis of depression'. It states that the partial or total depletion of catecholamines could result in depression.[1] The researchers go on to say that elation or mania (as in manic-depressive psychosis) could be caused by excessive supplies of catecholamines. In the same way, research has indicated that a depletion of the chemical serotonin (5-hydroxytryptamine or 5-HT) could cause depression. Other research[2] has shown a positive relationship between high levels of sodium and depression, and excessive amounts of steroids (17-hydrocorticoid) and suicide. Still further research[3] shows that endogenously depressed patients who no longer experience depression, had lower levels of sodium retention than those who still suffered from depression.

This type of research has been criticised, because the chemicals found in the bodies of depressed individuals could be present as a result of depression or they could occur together with depression, without being related to it[4].

More will be said about the chemical base of depression in Part 3 of this book dealing with psychotropic medication and depression.

The problem with explaining reactive depression as being due to external events occurs when a client is suffering from depression due to recent loss of a partner (through death or divorce) and displays psychotic behaviour or manic-depressive psychosis. This does not fit with the category of reactive depression in which there is not supposed to be psychotic (chemical) involvement.

During my research on depression, and for a short while in practice as a psychologist, I was against the idea of diagnosis of types of depression in terms of cause. I believed that depression should be described by what the therapist, client and the broader social system observed. I also believed that diagnosis should involve a description of how certain of the client's behaviour patterns within his or her family, social and work systems, as well as attitudes and behaviours of the therapist operated to keep the depressed person 'sick'. More will be said about this approach in Part 4 of this book, dealing with psychotherapy.

After years of practice with many depressed clients and their families, I still believe in the principles of my research. Experience has, however, softened my previous views. I now use a more inclusive approach to the description of depression, recognising hormonal factors, loss and past traumas, together with present dynamics within the various systems of the client.

A 19-year-old student consulted with me for severe depression. She had left university during her first year. She had hated her social science course. She was distressed to be causing her parents disappointment. She described how she had been withdrawing from her mother's intrusiveness. She was upset that her father was emotionally distant. Two of her best friends had been killed in motor accidents within the past six months. She had always suffered from severe premenstrual tension and depression, but the premenstrual period of distress had recently become extended from a few days to two weeks. Her parents reported that she was impossible to live with at that time. She had also recently been rejected by her boyfriend of long standing. There were obviously many factors deserving attention: recent loss – reactive depression, worsened premenstrual tension and depression and problematic family dynamics.

In this case I referred the client to a gynaecologist to treat her hormonal imbalance. We focused on her grief (deaths and the breakdown of her relationship). We also met with her family to negotiate appropriate boundaries of closeness and respect for each other's privacy. To diagnose this client in terms of one category would have been less than useful.

DEPRESSION AND STRESS

As mentioned earlier in this book, depression and stress are close companions, and in general present together. Prolonged stress also often triggers depression. The depressed person frequently complains of varying degrees of anxiety. The stressed client often presents with symptoms of depression. (An exception would be the person who is stressed from achieving or winning, or from some other positive source. Unless this person is 'burnt out' from this good stress – eustress – he or she doesn't usually experience associated depression.) For this reason, it would be helpful for the depressed client to complete the stress inventory that follows. As depression and stress are so contagious, it would be interesting for the person close to someone who is depressed also to complete this inventory.

STRESS QUESTIONNAIRE
Answer the following questions to find your level of stress. Choose one statement that best describes your response to each question.

Adapted from Looker and Gregson's *Assess your Stress* in *Stresswise* (1989)

1   You are upset by your partner's or colleague's behaviour. Do you:
    a   Blow up?
    b   Feel angry but suppress it?
    c   Feel upset, but do not get angry?
    d   Cry?
    e   None of the above?

2   *You must get through a mountain of work in one morning. Do you:*
    a   Work extra hard and complete the lot?
    b   Forget the work and make yourself a drink?
    c   Do as much as you can?
    d   Prioritise the load and complete only the important tasks?
    e   Ask someone to help you?

3   *You overhear a conversation in which a friend or colleague makes some unkind remarks about you. Do you:*
    a   Interrupt the conversation and give the person a piece of your mind?
    b   Walk straight by without giving the person much thought?
    c   Walk straight by and think about revenge?
    d   Walk straight by and think about them?

4   *You are stuck in heavy traffic. Do you:*
    a   Hoot?
    b   Try to drive down a side road to avoid the jam?
    c   Switch on the radio or cassette?
    d   Sit back and try to relax?
    e   Sit back and feel angry?
    f   Get on with some work?
    g   The question does not apply because you do not have a car?

5   *When you play a sport, do you play to win:*
    a   Always?
    b   Most of the time?
    c   Sometimes?
    d   Never. You play just for the game?

6   *When you play a game with children do you deliberately let them win:*
    a   Never. They've got to learn?
    b   Sometimes?
    c   Most of the time?
    d   Always. It is only a game?

7   *You are working on a project. The deadline is approaching fast, but the work is not quite right. Do you:*

a   Work on it night and day to make sure it's perfect?
   b   Start to panic because you think you will not complete it in time?
   c   Do your best in the time available without losing sleep over it?

8 *Someone regularly tidies up your room/office/garage/workshop and never puts the items/furniture in their original places. Do you:*
   a   Mark the position of each item and ask the person to put it back exactly where it should be?
   b   Move everything back to its original position after the person has gone?
   c   Leave most things as they are – you do not mind the occasional shift-round?

9 *A close friend asks you for your opinion about a newly-decorated room. Do you:*
   a   Think it's awful and say so?
   b   Think it's awful but say it looks wonderful?
   c   Think it's awful but comment on the good aspects?
   d   Think it's awful and suggest improvements?

10 *When you do something, do you:*
   a   Always work to produce a perfect result?
   b   Do your best and not worry if it is not perfect?
   c   Think that everything you do is perfect?

11 *Your family complains that you spend too little time with them because of work. Do you:*
   a   Worry but feel that you cannot do anything about it?
   b   Work in the lounge so that you can be with them?
   c   Take on more work?
   d   Find that your family has never complained?
   e   Reorganise your work so that you can be with them more?

12 *What is your idea of an ideal evening?*
   a   A large party with lots to drink and eat?
   b   An evening with your partner doing something you both enjoy?
   c   Getting away from it all by yourself?

    d   A small group of friends at dinner?
    e   An evening with the family doing things you all enjoy?
    f   Working?

13 *Which of the following do you do?*
    a   Bite your nails?
    b   Feel constantly tired?
    c   Feel breathless without exertion?
    d   Drum with your fingers?
    e   Sweat for no apparent reason?
    f   Fidget?
    g   Gesticulate?
    h   None of the above?

14 *Which of the following do you suffer from?*
    a   Headaches?
    b   Muscle tension?
    c   Constipation?
    d   Diarrhoea?
    e   Loss of appetite?
    f   Increase in appetite?
    g   None of the above?

15 *Have you experienced one or more of the following during the last month?*
    a   Cried or had the desire to cry?
    b   Found difficulty in concentration?
    c   Forgotten what you were going to say next?
    d   Little things irritated you?
    e   Found difficulty in making decisions?
    f   Wanted to scream?
    g   Felt that there is no one with whom you could really talk?
    h   Found that you have rushed on to another task before you have finished the first one?
    i   Have not experienced any of the above?

16 *Have you experienced any of the following during the last year?*
    a   A serious illness (yourself or someone close to you)?
    b   Problems with your family?
    c   Financial problems?

    d   None of the above?

17 *How many cigarettes do you smoke each day?*
    a   None?
    b   One to ten?
    c   Eleven to twenty?
    d   Twenty-one or more?

18 *How much alcohol do you drink a day?*
    a   None?
    b   One or two drinks?
    c   Three to five drinks?
    d   Six or more drinks?

19 *How many cups of freshly brewed (not decaffeinated) coffee do you drink a day?*
    a   None?
    b   One or two cups?
    c   Three to five cups?
    d   Six or more cups?

20 *How old are you?*
    a   18 or below?
    b   19 – 25?
    c   26 – 39?
    d   40 – 65?
    e   65 or over?

21 *You have a very important appointment at 9.30 a.m. Do you:*
    a   Have a sleepless night worrying about it?
    b   Sleep very well and wake up fairly relaxed, but thinking about the appointment?
    c   Sleep well and wake up looking forward to the appointment?

22 *Someone close to you has died. Of course you are very upset. Do you:*
    a   Grieve because no one can ever fill that awful gap?
    b   Grieve because life is so unfair?
    c   Accept what has happened and try to get on with your life?

23 *You have got into deep water over a problem. Do you:*
   a   Reassess the situation by yourself and try to find another solution?
   b   Talk over the problem with your partner or close friend and work something out?
   c   Deny that there is a problem in the hope that the worst will never happen?
   d   Worry about it but make no attempt to try and solve it?

24 *When did you last smile?*
   a   Today?
   b   Yesterday?
   c   Last week?
   d   Cannot remember?

25 *When did you last compliment or praise someone – your children, your partner, colleagues, friends?*
   a   Today?
   b   Yesterday?
   c   Last week?
   d   Cannot remember?

Scoring
Add up your score for each question:
   1   a = 0   b = 0   c = 3   d = 0   e = 1
   2   a = 1   b = 0   c = 1   d = 3   e = 2
   3   a = 0   b = 3   c = 0   d = 1
   4   a = 0   b = 2   c = 2   d = 3   e = 0   f = 2   g = 1
   5   a = 0   b = 1   c = 2   d = 3
   6   a = 0   b = 1   c = 2   d = 3
   7   a = 0   b = 0   c = 3
   8   a = 0   b = 0   c = 3
   9   a = 0   b = 0   c = 3   d = 1
   10 a = 0   b = 3   c = 0
   11 a = 0   b = 0   c = 0   d = 0   e = 3
   12 a = 1   b = 3   c = 0   d = 1   e = 2   f = 0
   13 a = 0   b = 0   c = 0   d = 0   e = 0   f = 0   g = 0   h = 1
   14 a = 0   b = 0   c = 0   d = 0   e = 0   f = 0   g = 0
   15 a = 0   b = 0   c = 0   d = 0   e = 0   f = 0   g = 0   h = 0   i = 1
   16 a = 0   b = 0   c = 0   d = 2

17 a = 3   b = 1   c = 0   d = 0
18 a = 3   b = 2   c = 1   d = 0
19 a = 3   b = 2   c = 1   d = 0
20 a = 0   b = 0   c = 1   d = 2   e = 3
21 a = 0   b = 1   c = 3
22 a = 0   b = 0   c = 3
23 a = 2   b = 3   c = 0   d = 0
24 a = 3   b = 2   c = 1   d = 0
25 a = 3   b = 2   c = 1   d = 0

Your score

51 – 68

Your stress level is low. You show very few signs of stress. You are not a workaholic. You thus show Type B behaviour and generally cope very well with stress.

33 – 50

Your stress level is moderate. You show some stress. You are not a workaholic but there is some tendency towards it. You therefore show mild Type A behaviour and generally cope quite well with stress.

16 – 32

Your stress level is high. You show many signs of stress. It is likely that you are a workaholic. You thus display moderate Type A behaviour and do not handle stress very well.

0 – 15

Your stress level is very high. You show a great deal of stress. You are a workaholic. You display extreme Type A behavior and your ability to deal with stress is very poor.

SUMMARY

In this section depression has been described from the depressed person's point of view. Creative methods (clay modelling with music and story telling), and quantitative means (depression inventory) have been used. An attempt has also been made to assist those close to a depressed person to understand how it feels to be depressed – if they are not experiencing depression already.

In addition, information has been provided (albeit controversial) on types and causes of depression. The presence of stress with depression has been highlighted. A stress inventory and its scoring has been recommended to assess the level of stress being experienced.

WHAT IS IT LIKE FOR YOU TO BE CLOSELY ASSOCIATED WITH A DEPRESSED PERSON?

This person may be:

- your spouse
- your lover
- your parent
- your child
- your sibling
- your friend
- your work associate
- your employer
- your employee

In this section, there is a shift in emphasis from the perspective of the depressed person to those closely associated with the depressed individual.

First, a case study from my files is presented. This is followed by my recommending that you make a collage to show the quality of your feeling about how it feels to be closely associated with a depressed person. The depressed reader is also asked to make a collage, visualising how it must feel for those close to him or her. Then, as with the section describing the depressed person's view of depression, you will be asked to write your story of how it feels to associate with a depressed individual.

THE STORY OF GINA

Thinking about this section, I remembered Gina, 40, who consulted with me about five years ago. She had finally left her husband, Nick, 47, after a marriage of 20 years. They had two children, a son and a daughter – both adolescents. Nick had suffered from severe episodes of depression, interspersed with periods of mania, and Gina had finally had enough. This is her story.

'I met Nick when I was still at school. He was so gorgeous – tall, handsome and the oldest guy I'd ever dated. I was on holiday with my parents in his home town. I saw him and fell in love. I was 17 years old, and he was 24. He seemed to know so much about life, and seemed so wise. I told my parents, after our first meeting, that I was going to marry Nick.

'We corresponded during my last year of school. He was charming and related well to my father, always adding a postscript filled with humour for my dad, to his letters. I left school and moved to his hometown to study. He was supportive of my pursuits and career ambitions. After a few false starts, I realised that law was my vocation. He, too, was studying and we would talk daily on the telephone, and spend every weekend together.

'Life was great. I felt so secure knowing that I had a steady boyfriend. His family was wonderful to me, especially his mother. From time to time, however, I would become a bit confused. Nick would not talk civilly to his parents. He called his mother a "bitch" and thought that his father was stupid. His mother would cook delicious food that he would refuse to eat.

'He identified with my father who was well-educated and kept asking me to ask my dad for money and contacts. My mother irritated him. It bothered me that Nick would become moody, sometimes for days on end. At those times he would not speak to me.

'Throughout our relationship and marriage, no reference was ever made to the term "depression". "Moody" and "bad mood" were used. When he eventually got over a mood, he would tell me that he had been cross because of something that I or someone else had said or done. For example, he called his brother "a bastard" for some comment that he had made months ago. He wouldn't speak to his cousin because his cousin's parents had promised Nick a holiday while he was still at school, but had not carried through their promise. I would sometimes forget my keys to the place where I was staying, and this would provoke great anger, followed by long periods of moodiness. Between times Nick would be cheerful, full of energy and he would initiate great adventures. He made me very happy during the "up" times, and very confused and upset during the "down" times. I thought that his moods would improve if I could do certain things to make him happy: stay thin, cook well, never forget anything.

'The hardest for me was that he kept failing courses at university. He desperately wanted to get accepted into a post-graduate business degree, but because of his academic record, both at high school and while studying for his under-graduate degree, he was constantly being rejected for admission to post-graduate studies around the country and overseas. When the letters of refusal arrived, he would go into a deep, dark slump. I would be in a state of nerves. At these times I could do nothing right. He told me that my father should be able to get him into a business school through his contacts in high places. My father certainly tried, but Nick's record of failure prevented his being admitted. Nick suggested that I should visit the deans of various business schools and persuade them that he was a good choice for the course. In my naive way I did so, first dressing as smartly as I could to give the right impression. What a stupid, unassertive wimp I was in those days! Who did I think I was, to bear this heavy burden? I kept thinking that it was up to me to make Nick happy. If I didn't he would continue to be miserable, make me miserable and life would be hell! My worst nightmare was that Nick might leave me if I did not make things "right" for him. My feelings vacillated between sympathy for him and confusion. I did not believe that I was a bad person but he was pretty convincing. If I did not fix things for him, I was as bad as the "others" who made his life difficult. Confusion, confusion, confusion. My stomach would be in a tight knot whenever Nick was in a mood. Then I would get carried away with immense pleasure and joy when he was on a high. Life would be so exciting. I had a nagging fear that his mood would descend again if I did not do something to keep him happy.

'On the few occasions that I became angry with Nick, and where he could not persuade me that it was my fault, he had an incredible ability to humour me out of my anger – all would be forgiven.

'I had always wanted to get married while still a virgin. It was so wonderful that Nick respected my wishes. He occasionally asked me to help him masturbate, but otherwise showed no sexual desire for me during the three years that we dated.

'I realised on our honeymoon that neither of us had ever had sex. It was a disaster. He was angry that I did not know how to move during intercourse. I experienced pain the first time, due to being a virgin. Nick was far from gentle. In the next few years he would want sex with me only in summer, after I had cultivated a dark tan, and even then, only occasionally.

'Nick would say: "Let's have a screw. Are you ready?" No foreplay. No words of endearment. After he had released and relieved himself, he would roll over and go to sleep. I did not experience any pleasure from this activity. I was not physically attracted to Nick. I did feel a sexual attraction to men whom I knew, like my boss who was kind and attentive to me. I never told anyone about this attraction. I definitely did not believe in having an affair outside of marriage.

'I look back now and wonder where my sexuality was hiding. He used to tell me that I looked sexy when I was underweight. I seemed to lose weight when he was in a bad mood. He told me that he needed to be difficult so that I could stay thin. He encouraged me to wear revealing clothes and enjoyed it if other men looked at me or commented on my figure. He was revolted by fat women. I suffered severe headaches and spastic colon attacks. Nick was good to me when I was sick.

'Our respective families were overjoyed when we got married. Nick was studying those courses he had failed at night and working a full day as an estate agent. Our friends included only those people who were potential buyers or sellers of property. I also worked a full day and studied at night for my law degree. My role also consisted of doing all the cooking and cleaning of our apartment. We had hired a part-time char-lady. Nick liked to sit and wait to be served. The food had to be gourmet-style. If the texture, taste or quality of the food was not perfect, Nick would descend into a black sulk. He would sit down for a meal and ask me where I had bought the food, how much seasoning I had added and the method I had used to cook his dinner. My stomach would be in a knot in anticipation of the questions. On the one occasion that the potato chips had been too light in colour, he threw his plate of veal schnitzel, peas and lightly-coloured potato chips against the wall. The plate had smashed and the mess lay on the freshly-polished wooden floor. He had stormed off into the bedroom. This mood had lasted for longer than a week. After this he would come home to my carefully prepared meals, not speak to me but go straight to our bedroom and go to sleep. I had spent those nights in the spare room in a state of nerves. I kept wondering how I could improve my cooking to keep him happy. In better times he would come home from work in a tense mood. He would look around the apartment and find some dust or a spider-web that I had missed. He would then either scream: "You fucking lazy bitch", or tell me about the dirt in an abrupt manner. In both instances he would go to bed in a black mood. The moods would be worse when he had failed to conclude a property sale, or when he had failed a course.

'When Nick was in a bad mood his face would change from amiable, smiling and warm, to pale with whiteness around his mouth. His eyes would go glassy and look venomous. I would be terrified, but told no-one.

'He had insisted that I ask for an increase in salary at work at intervals of about four to five months. I was happy in my job and felt embarrassed at frequently asking for an increase.

'He would also regularly tell me to ask my parents for money to help with expenses. I would avoid that. My style was to give and not to take from people. I hated asking for favours from anyone.

'I fell pregnant about 18 months after we were married yet Nick continued to demand the same level of service at home.

'Three days before our first baby was due to be born my father died suddenly of a heart attack. I had been at our home with Nick when the call had come to tell us that my dad had died. He had been my hero and the best father that any daughter could wish for. He was gone. I was 23. He had wanted grandchildren desperately. I sobbed like a small child. I had lost my rock. Nick was comforting. He had adored my father and he cried also. To go home would have meant a long aeroplane trip for me. My doctor advised me against going home. Nick wanted to go to the funeral but my mother had sent a message asking him to stay with me as the baby was almost due. He was angry with her for controlling his movements. He went into another bad mood – this time only for a short while. Nick left the apartment to go and buy some tranquillisers that had been prescribed by my gyneacologist. I was at home on my own crying and feeling so lonely. My char-lady arrived. I told her what had happened. She was concerned and insisted that I stop crying, that it was very bad for the baby. I stopped crying and for nine years pushed my mourning inward.

'I was in a state of shock at my loss. The birth of our baby so soon after my beloved father had died felt like another shock. I felt that this was another shock. He was a healthy little boy, but I did not know how to cope. My mother arrived the day after our son was born. She and my dad had been planning to come to help me with the baby, as they had done for my sister when she had her first child. My mother looked pale and somehow in another world. I realised that, not only would I have to cope with our son on my own, but I would need to be strong for my mother as well. My mother and sister went back to my hometown to pack my mother's things, sell her house and move her into our home.

'I went home from the nursing home with the baby to a complete mess. Washing was all over the bed in our baby son's room, dirty dishes were piled in the kitchen sink and no meal was prepared. I took the baby to the supermarket to do the shopping but felt faint. I grabbed a few essentials and went home. What followed felt like a nightmare. Our baby son seemed to be uncomfortable and colicky most of the time. I did not know what to do to make him more comfortable. I read Dr. Spock from cover to cover, and wore out the chapter on "crying". I telephoned my mother-in-law for advice often and cried a lot myself.

'Nick still demanded the gourmet meals and spotless house. His moodiness had increased. When our baby cried or was restless, Nick became more and more sullen. He would throw things, slam doors, wear earmuffs and sometimes go to his office at 3 a.m. I kept wishing that Nick would disappear because I knew that things would be easier if I could relax and get to know my baby.

'I would make sure meals were ready on time in the evenings when Nick walked in, although the baby was crying from colic. Nick would storm off to the bedroom and refuse to eat. I took to sleeping in the spare room with the baby, with my foot on his pram, rocking him to and fro, or sitting on the bed holding him so that he would not disturb Nick and send him into a mood. I became exhausted from lack of sleep and from living in fear in a tense atmosphere. My baby could feel my distress. He was not a contented baby – how could he be?

'When our son was still tiny we moved into a new house. My mother and her beloved poodle moved in with us. She was having a "nervous breakdown". Her dog had to stay inside except for walks a couple of times a day. My mother wanted five tasty meals a day. Her dog vomited and defecated on the carpet, probably due to the terrible vibe in the house. The baby was still restless. Nick would leave for work in a black mood, and when he arrived home noticed not only the dust on the mantelpiece (of which there now was more), but the spider webs and the dog's mess as well. He said, "Your mother goes, or I go!"

'He also still wanted the fancy meals and quiet while he was studying. I was trying to study too. My body and mind seemed to seize up after two months of his moods, my mother crying on my one shoulder and my baby on the other. I no longer knew how to please everyone. I had lost an enormous amount of weight, and all I wanted to do was to stand in the main road and get run over by a truck! I lay on my bed one afternoon and could not move. I felt like a piece of cement. My sister visited, took one look at me and took my mother to stay with her. I did not tell her about Nick. I thought then about talking to my doctor, but decided not to. I threw myself into my studies. My mother moved into her own home, but the ups and downs continued.

'I was doing well in my studies and Nick was still encouraging me in this regard, as long as the house ran smoothly. I employed full-time domestic help. This helped enormously. Our son was growing up and, while very shy, was less of a screamer. I told Nick, "No more children. I will not be able to cope with you and with another baby's screaming." He said that if I did not have another child he would divorce me.

'We spent most nights in separate rooms. He said that I breathed too loudly and disturbed him when I slept next to him, or when I turned over in bed. We did, however, manage to conceive a second child, on one of the rare occasions that we had sex in the hot, suntanned months.

'Our second baby, a daughter, was born just after I had earned my first degree. Nick also graduated before our daughter was born. I prayed that this child would be quiet. She was. Our wonderful domestic helper would carry the baby on her back if she became noisy when Nick was home.

'Our home-life was unpredictable. It could be fun, with both of us romping with the children, or reading to them, or making puzzles or baking with them. Or, for some small reason the peaceful scene would erupt, with Nick going to his room in a huff after screaming at me or one of the children. The children learnt very early to say, "Daddy's in a bad mood."

'Things were very tight financially. Besides caring for the children, organising the home and studying for further qualifications, I worked part-time at Nick's office. I also ran my own home industry with a neighbour. Nick told all his business associates how proud he was of me, and how I was his long-term financial investment. He said that he wanted to retire once I had qualified. Then he would study for a MBA. Nick would either be wonderful to me at his office or totally piggish – the latter when I moved one of his office chairs slightly or forgot something minor. This would trigger days of his black moods. Despite our financial position, Nick would buy his clients expensive gifts (garden furniture, music centres and Mixmasters). We regularly had our telephone and electricity cut off. Once this happened the day before my final exam. I said nothing and studied by candlelight.

'Nick frequently bought motor cars on hire purchase – at one time we had three – but we did not have enough money for groceries.

'At about this time we had one of our infrequent sex sessions. I had a series of orgasms, seemingly from oral sex. This was the first time that Nick had performed oral sex on me and the first time that I had experienced orgasms with him. That was the last time that Nick touched me.

'When he was in a good mood, Nick was the most wonderful father. At these times he said that I looked beautiful. When he was in a bad mood I looked repulsive to him and the children's activities irritated him. Our children were now coming home from school during Nick's frequent and prolonged bad moods, and immediately asking, "Is daddy still in a bad mood?" If he was, they would be subdued and tense. If he was in a good mood they would have fun with him.

'I tried to make social arrangements with friends and their husbands. Frequently Nick would arrive home in a bad mood and tell me to cancel the arrangement. I did.

'Once I had qualified as a lawyer and completed my articles, I decided to do my pupilage for the Bar. I was accepted as an advocate at the Supreme Court Bar. Friends and family wanted to celebrate with us. An elderly couple came from my hometown for the occasion. Nick was the perfect husband – hospitable and taking photographs of me with my family, friends and children. He told everyone that he could now retire and study full time. However, no university would accept him with his poor academic record. I felt sorry for him. The elderly couple who had always been close to me had phoned to say that they would be extending their stay. I invited them for dinner. That afternoon my six-year-old daughter had spilt juice on the carpet.

'Nick lost control and beat her senseless for being so careless. Our domestic helper said that she was leaving as she could not watch a young child being punished so unnecessarily. Nick told me to cancel dinner. I had to explain to these wonderful friends why our dinner was cancelled. I went to meet them at my mother's apartment. She took the children for a walk and a milkshake while I talked and cried and talked some more. This was the first time that outsiders had learned about Nick's depression and the struggle that I and my children had been going through.

'I had been hurt and angered so often that I gradually stopped feeling sorry for Nick. I stopped caring for him and I stopped wanting to please him. I was concerned for the wellbeing of the children in this tense, unpredictable atmosphere. At the same time, I was worried about the effects of divorce on them. I nevertheless decided to leave. Nick was served with divorce papers. His reaction was to become completely different. He came crying to me and the children. He apologised for what he had done to us and promised to change. I felt dead inside. I felt nothing. However, he persuaded me to go with him for counselling, and for eight months our home was peaceful. Nick had no bad moods. It was a miracle. We had people over for dinner and I felt happy. We talked a lot. There was one worrying aspect though: Nick would still not touch me. I tried to seduce him – no response. He told me that sex was not important to him. I decided that if our home was free from the terrible fear, moods and tension, I was prepared to forgo sex. Our children were relaxed and blossoming. We explored new and beautiful places every weekend and life was great!

'This miracle lasted for about eight months after which Nick dropped a bombshell: "You are walking around as if you own the place. You have become hard. You think you can feed the people who come here on money that I slave every day to earn. I want things the way they were. I want you to give me all the money you earn, and I don't want anyone to visit us at home – I can't afford it." He continued, "You know that I married you as a long-term financial investment, and you are not playing the game." I challenged him by explaining that I gave him three-quarters of my income, and marriage should not be based on financial support. "What about emotional support, caring, making love and things other than money?" I asked. He told me that money was the only support he wanted. I was shocked. I felt confused and desperate. I felt such incredible hatred for this man. I remember getting into my car and driving along the highway. I was crying and could not see properly. I didn't care if I smashed into a car – I didn't care about anything. I could no longer risk my sanity in that madhouse. I sued for divorce.

'Nick attacked me physically for the first time when I refused to support him financially through a Master's degree. He pulled chunks of my hair out and fumbled for the kitchen knives. Nick could not understand why I was leaving. He wanted custody of the children and most of the assets. Because of the custody issue, we both had to be assessed by psychologists and a psychiatrist, with and without the children. At the end of this, both psychologists and the psychiatrist reported that Nick had a personality disorder with severe depression, and that he should be on antidepressants. He refused this treatment, saying that there was nothing wrong with him.

'Five years later, I feel reborn. Life is great. I have a wonderful relationship with a kind and honest man, but I don't think that I will ever get married again. I have flashbacks to the upheavals, unpredictability, vacillating feelings of sympathy and explosive anger towards Nick and those black, tense moods which I now understand are part of depression. I also realise that I caught Nick's depression and for a long time was disempowered and immobilised by it. My son and daughter see their father and comment that they feel depressed when they have spent an evening with him. They do, however, still feel sorry for him. I never see him, nor do I want to.'

SYMPTOMS OF THOSE CLOSELY ASSOCIATED WITH A DEPRESSED PERSON

Gina experienced many of the feelings that those close to a depressed person feel:

- a futile wish to help
- feelings that vacillate between sympathy and frustration
- desperation
- fear and sometimes terror
- entrapment
- tension
- depression

- disempowerment
- being depended upon
- being blamed unfairly
- physical ailments: headaches, stomach aches, frequent viruses
- social isolation
- needing to adopt a brave face for the outside world
- insecurity
- a wish to tell the 'patient' to pull himself or herself together
- taking the role of 'caretaker' or 'family therapist'
- feeling like a helpless child but needing to act responsibly
- anxiety that people might invite them out as a couple or family – and how to refuse these invitations
- exhaustion
- fear of leaving
- hope that the 'up' times will last if only one could do something to make him or her feel better.

The pain of those close to a depressed person is frequently missed or ignored. The emphasis is placed on the depressed person. Close associates mostly need to cope with the depressed person and put their own, frequently ambivalent feelings on hold.

COLLAGE

I ask those readers who are close to a depressed person to make a collage. Readers who are depressed will also benefit from this activity.

You will need the following materials:

- your favourite music
- a large sheet of plain paper
- some old magazines
- glue
- some coloured felt-tipped pens or crayons
- scissors

Switch on your favourite music. Visualise how it feels to associate with a depressed person. Don't analyse, just relax. Page through some old magazines and tear or cut out pictures, words, poems or anything that appeals to you. Paste these on the plain sheet of paper. Do not worry about neatness. You may draw in between the pasted pictures and/or words. Get in touch with the music. You may draw stick figures or write poetry or words of your own, or anything you wish. This is not a pretty picture to hang on the wall – it is an expression of how you are feeling. You may even choose to use tomato sauce, mustard, Worcestershire sauce or other condiments that appeal!

When you have finished, look at your collage. It will help you to understand how you are feeling about your life. If you are the depressed person, you will most probably have a clearer understanding of how those close to you experience your depression.

Of greatest benefit would be for both people to make a collage, and to explain your respective collages to each other. If it is not possible to explain your collage to someone who is closely associated with you, then tell a friend whom you trust, or talk your interpretation into a tape recorder and play it back to yourself.

My clients and participants in my workshops have been astounded at the way in which they create, and thereby clarify, their experiences by means of collage. This is a right-brain (subconscious) activity that taps into emotions that reside deep inside of you. It is important to release these by bringing them to consciousness and by talking about them.

WRITE OR TELL YOUR STORY

You have thus far looked at depression from the depressed person's point of view. You have read the story of Gina and Nick, at the start of this section, and you have creatively described your experience of close association with a depressed person by means of a collage.

I ask you now to write or tell your story. If you are writing, use your non-dominant hand. As explained in the first section, this releases deep-seated emotions. If you would prefer to tell your story, talk to a trusted person or to the depressed person who is close to you. If such a person is unavailable, physically or emotionally, talk your story onto a blank audio cassette.

Start by describing your present situation, then go back as far as you can remember in your life. Describe your childhood, your parents (in relation to each other and to you), your siblings, your schooling and friends, your relationships (and marriage/s, and/or divorce/s), your work-history, your children, grandchildren, in-laws, finances, holidays, socialising and any other aspect of your life that comes to mind. At the end of your story you will feel tired, perhaps exhausted. You may feel anxious, tearful and/or extremely angry. As happened when you made the collage, you will have remembered incidents and emotions that have been locked deep inside of you. This process is cleansing and healing. You will feel open and vulnerable for a few hours or a few days – this is positive. It is important for you to care for yourself at this time, as you would for a small, defenceless child. Do exercise, relax, listen to soothing music, cry if you want to and allow yourself to continue to feel the good, the bad and the painful. To feel is to be alive.

SUMMARY

This section has been an attempt to describe depression from the perspective of those close to a depressed person. I hope that the depressed reader has benefited from this section by gaining greater insight and empathy into the experience of those close to him or her.
   Strong emphasis has been placed on creativity (the collage, music, storytelling) so that the process of explaining and describing is also the process of healing by releasing deep-seated emotions.

THE THERAPIST'S DESCRIPTION OF DEPRESSION

In this section, I invite you, the reader, to enter my head for a while and to look at depression from my perspective. I shall be using the case studies in the earlier sections of the book to illustrate my views. I shall also be drawing on vignettes from clients I have seen over the years.
   When I first meet with a new client I look at physical appearance, facial expressions and interactions between people in a depressed system. I listen to what each person has to say, I listen to their tones of voice and watch other non-verbal expressions of their problems. I ask many questions about present, past and future perceptions. I also ask about other people who exist in the client's and their families' lives. I sometimes work with these other

people. I ask about work and study. I listen and look some more. I make sure to ask for positive aspects in the client's life and reinforce these positive perceptions.

Please follow me in my exploration of depression. Agree or disagree, and add your own comments, interpretations and explanations. We are all going to benefit if you become as involved in what follows as you were in what went before.

HOW DOES THE THERAPIST DESCRIBE THE DEPRESSED CLIENT?

Think back to the case of Rob and Sara.

I had listened to the referring doctor describe Rob as 'non-coping'. He could not understand how Rob had advanced so far and so fast in his career. The doctor told me how Rob sobbed like a baby in his consulting rooms.

What I observed when I visited Rob was as follows:

- He was unshaven.
- His eyes were glassy and seemed dead.
- His face was pale.
- His movements were slow.
- He looked like someone in shock.
- He looked like someone in pain.
- He showed signs of high anxiety.
- He looked confused and terrified.

I listened to the following:

- Rob's tone of voice was flat and monotonous.
- I heard him blaming and castigating himself.
- I heard him describe himself as a failure.
- I also listened to him talk about his quick move up the corporate ladder, and the success and confidence he felt in his previous career direction and the shock of finding himself working in a different direction. I heard him when he explained how the new direction was the way to go in his company for future growth. I heard how he rationalised that, if he moved back to where he was, there would soon be a ceiling in his growth.
- I listened carefully to Rob's belief in his own competence and confidence in his previous area of growth and his uncomfortable 'gut-feel' about his present career path.

- I heard how Rob's style was one of compliance and submission to authority, and how he would ignore his 'gut' intuition in favour of what others told him was the correct way to go.
- Most of my clients call me 'Sue'. Rob called me 'Dr. Musikanth'. I was the authority, despite the fact that I had invited him to call me 'Sue'.
- With further questioning, I established that there was another career direction in which Rob could go that involved the kind of work he enjoyed. This path had the potential for limitless growth. His voice became strong and his face lit up when he talked of it. He had never felt that he had had the right to 'sell himself' to top management for the career direction that he wanted. He was not comfortable asserting himself.
- I heard Rob talk of the illness and death of his father many years before, and I heard a man still in deep mourning.
- I heard guilt and recrimination because he was unable to save his father from the pain of cancer.
- I heard a person who wanted to please and who was trying to be all things to all people (again inassertive).
- I heard how Rob had tried to protect his mother from the hardships of nursing his father. He had insisted that his father stay in hospital rather than go home. His father had begged to be allowed to go home.
- I listened to Rob's guilt at having kept his father's impending death to himself. He had made the decision not to tell his mother that his father was terminally ill. He had not thought his mother could cope with that news. He had also decided not to tell his father that he was dying. When his father had tried to talk of death and dying, Rob had given him messages of wellness and good health. In retrospect, Rob felt he had made a huge mistake in keeping the bad news from his parents.
- I heard Rob tell me that he had previously experienced physical symptoms of stress but never depression. With my next questions to Rob and Sara, I learned that Rob had been displaying a depressive style of behaviour at home for as long as he or Sara could remember: avoidance of social contacts (except after sport, and then only when he had had a good deal to drink). Sara described his behaviour on these occasions as loud with foul language and a rude attitude towards her. In general, he had been quiet at home. He watched an inordinate amount of

television. He had struggled to sleep more than a few hours every night and his appetite was poor. He had not made love with Sara for months. She explained how when he had become very depressed, there had been no sexual activity between them.

When Rob came out of hospital, I met with him, Sara and his superior at Head Office.

At this meeting Rob's boss described him as having been exceptionally competent in his previous position. He did, however, say that Rob was a perfectionist with obsessive attention to detail. I watched Rob become submissive, anxious and apologetic for letting the company down.

From this case study and the many depressed clients with whom I have consulted, I have seen and heard patterns that include the following:

- down-in-the-mouth
- pale complexion
- dull eyes
- head in hands
- slow movements
- hunched shoulders
- monotonous tone of voice
- poor self-esteem
- feelings of failure
- dependent behaviour
- sadness
- inassertiveness
- self-blame
- high anxiety, fear and even terror
- inability to cope
- poor self-confidence
- self-involvement (narcissistic behaviour)
- feelings of inferiority
- neglect of appearance
- embarrassment at feeling depressed

Take a blank sheet of paper and head it: *What would I see or hear when faced with a depressed person?* Jot down the verbal and non-verbal behaviours that you have seen or are likely to see.

How does the therapist describe those close to the depressed client?

Remember the story of Gina? She took responsibility for curing Nick's moods:
If only she could cook better....
If only she could get him into Graduate Business School...
If she remained thin...
If she could produce quiet babies....
If only she could earn more money...

I heard Gina take on the role of the 'sympathetic caretaker'. By means of all of the above pursuits and thoughts, she believed that she could make Nick better.

While she talked, I heard not only the sympathy in her tone of voice, but also the enormous anger and frustration. I heard her immobilised by these diametrically opposed feelings. She was not used to expressing anger, but it was written all over her face and was evident in her body language:

- She clenched her fists.
- She spoke in an angry tone of voice.

This was especially so when she spoke of Nick's unpredictable and sometimes cruel interactions with her children. She displayed many of the symptoms of depression and stress that she had contracted in her tense and depressed family:

- high levels of anxiety
- constant, debilitating headaches
- frequent viruses
- poor self-esteem
- guilt
- self-blame
- inability to say no
- feeling of failure
- exhaustion
- despair
- immobilisation

The interesting paradox with Gina was how she glowed and sparkled when she spoke of her studies and her work:

- She loved what she was doing.
- She gained immense satisfaction from winning cases for her clients.
- She enjoyed interacting with her colleagues and clerical staff. Of interest was the fact that she never expressed pride in her accomplishments or patted herself on the back for what she had coped with in the face of great adversity.
- She subtly put herself down or gave others credit for her achievements: 'Nick gave me the support to study.' 'I am lucky to have such understanding children.' 'My mother and mother-in-law have helped me by looking after the children.' 'I could not have managed without my wonderful domestic helper...'

Whilst some might have thought Gina a wimp and a weakling to have put up with Nick's behaviour, I viewed her as a brave woman. She did not have a road map for the kind of life in which she found herself. She stoically tried every avenue available to her to remedy the situation. When she slowly realised that she could do nothing to help Nick with his depression and that his moods had not been her fault, and when she had built the confidence to like herself and protect herself – she left.

Think for a while about what you would see and hear when faced with a person who is close to a depressed person. Take a blank sheet of paper and head it: *Behaviour patterns of those close to a depressed person*. Jot down the verbal and non-verbal behaviours that you have seen or are likely to see.

The following are general patterns that I have observed and heard from clients who are closely associated with a depressed person:

- a strong need to cure the depression
- sympathetic caretaker
- tough-talking caretaker ('pull yourself together')
- social isolation
- over-compensation and over-protection of victimised children
- inability to say 'no'
- neglect of own emotional needs

- suppression of sexual needs
- frustration and/or anger alternating with or simultaneous with sympathy
- embarrassment if 'outsiders' should notice the depression
- assumption of a superior psychological position
- placing the depressed person into an inferior psychological position – that of 'ill patient'
- displaying symptoms of depression and stress in reaction to the depressed person's behaviour

How does the therapist experience psychotherapy with a depressed client and those close to a depressed client?

I shall give you an example of two therapeutic encounters with depression (a depressed client and someone close to a depressed person).

Therapeutic connection with depression
Think back to the story of Jenny – a depressed client's description of depression. I observed and heard her symptoms, typical of depression. These included: lethargy, weepiness, lack of motivation for work, withdrawal from friends, loss of appetite, sleep disturbance, retarded motor activity, anxiety, pale complexion and self-involvement. I saw a severely depressed client who had, until now, coped with an extremely pathological, alcoholic and violent family system. I worked with Jenny to relive her painful childhood and to face the guilt she felt at the violent murder of her father. I was amazed at her strength and courage in the face of so much adversity. I wondered how she had come out of this comparatively normal. I told Jenny that I was not confident that I would have remained so balanced, given her on-going psychological and physical life crises.

We worked with the past and present and with her future aspirations. Jenny's focus moved and grew. She took the initiative. She disentangled herself emotionally from the pathology in her family. She started to exercise regularly. She reconnected with special friends and strengthened her bond with her brother. She took up part-time catering, thus filling her financial coffers. She lightened and blossomed. I felt proud of her and she felt proud of herself. I felt a little like a good mother to Jenny. I encouraged her independence and taught her how to listen to her gut instinct as well as her head when making decisions. I had helped her to have the confidence to say NO! to unreasonable requests. By the end of our therapy she had met a kind, loving man but, most important, she had learnt how to nurture and mother herself. She would still give of herself in relationships, but had learned how to take caring and love for herself as well.

This connection with a depressed client feels good for me as therapist.

What follows is my description of therapy with Gina, who was married to a depressed person...

Gina consulted with me at the end of her marriage to Nick. The strongest feeling I had with Gina was that it was the perfect time for therapy. She had worked on her decision to leave for a long time before consulting with me. I saw a combination of excitement at the prospect of a new life and anticipation of peace of mind, without moods or depression or fear. Her greatest fear was that Nick might somehow sabotage her peace. Her Achille's heel was her children. She struck me as intelligent, articulate, warm and caring. Despite the abuse to which she had been subjected in her marriage, she continued to wish Nick well – albeit far away from her. Therapy with Gina involved storytelling and collage-making together with conversation between us. I offered her practical guidelines for single parenting that would be compatible with her system (family, friends, values and the children's particular scholastic and personality needs).

I watched Gina set the pace that suited her for therapy. She listened to me and to others, but moved at a speed that was right for her. She expressed a feeling of safety in therapy that allowed her to experience and release enormous anger and pain. Gina used me as the base from which she could take the steps of her journey. Once I had met Nick, in connection with their custody battle, I suggested to him that he enter therapy to work through his own issues.

He said, 'There is nothing wrong with me. I do not need help.'

I do not believe in pushing clients into therapy. Gina was motivated and ready to address her issues. Nick was not.

From Gina's perspective, therapy helped her to clear away strong, frightening feelings.

She also told me, 'You are strong enough even for me. You talk common sense and provide me with a road map for myself and my children which I feel free to follow in my own time. You give me respect and reassurance. I look forward to the future and I know that you will always be there for me when I feel the need.'

The connection with Gina gave me an 'up' feeling. It was a privilege to walk the last part of her journey with her.

My clients and those close to them are my teachers – they are experts in the arena of life. Combine their learning with my perceptions and experience and we have a delicious recipe for growth and development – theirs and mine!

SUMMARY

In this section I have asked you to look at, and listen to, depression through my eyes and ears as if you were the therapist.

Part 1 of this book has described and examined depression from the following perspectives:

- the depressed client
- those closely associated with a depressed person
- the therapist's description of depression

PART 2

SELF-HELP AND DEPRESSION

Part 1 of this book describes depression. By your connection with me in that description, you have started to help yourself by:

- storytelling
- the making of collages
- clay modelling

What follows includes all of those, and offers a variety of other ways to manage depression. These include:

- exercise
- deep muscle relaxation
- creativity
- humour
- positive thinking and more

These self-help methods may be used before seeking professional help. I have also found them to be successful in combination with the existing professional approaches to depression. This inclusive approach will become evident in the following parts of this book:

- medical (Part 3)
- psychotherapeutic (Part 4)
- holistic (Part 5)

These skills will benefit you, the reader, whether you are the depressed person or are close to someone who is depressed. While the focus is on helping yourself in a depressed system, the skills that follow will help to achieve a balanced lifestyle for everyone!

Exercise

NB Please consult with your medical doctor before commencing any exercise program.

Why is this the first skill that I discuss? Why does it have such a large heading?
Because it works!
      it works!
         it works!

Who says so?

Depressed clients
My doctoral research was a study of the treatment of depression. For this I needed to interview many hundreds of depressed people, and conduct psychotherapy sessions with some of them. I heard about the benefits of exercise for depression over and over again.

Since the end of that research, in 1985, I have consulted with thousands of stressed and depressed clients. They too report on how exercise makes them feel: happier, more relaxed, better able to concentrate, more positive, more energetic and generally less depressed.

Brenda, 22, a final-year Fine Art student was referred to me by one of her lecturers with severe depressive symptomatology. We worked together in therapy, where she came to trust her gut instincts and where she could go down into a 'dark place' and not panic that she would remain depressed. This is a common fear of people who go into a depression from time to time. We worked through the recent breakdown of a long-standing relationship. Her ex-boyfriend had left when he could neither understand nor 'fix' her depression. We terminated therapy when Brenda had sufficient insight and the skills to adequately manage her 'up-and-down' periods.

Brenda telephoned me some nine months after our last session to tell me that she was fine. We decided to meet for a talk. She had been so impressed with the effects of exercise on her mind (and body) that she had gone on to complete an aerobic instructor's course.

She said; 'My head is uncluttered. My body looks great. My confidence is way up. I hardly go into "downs" at all any more. When I do, I just go with the flow. I feel much more positive and I have not thought of suicide once since we last consulted. I am still creating wonderful art and I write regularly. I will never stop exercising because it seems to have played a major role in releasing me from my terrifying depression.'

It often happens that clients who consult me for depression report that they have given up regular exercise. In conversation with them I learn that from the time they stopped exercising they have felt worse, or they tell me that their depression started at about that time. They also tell me that they felt better when they were exercising. This is the feedback that I have heard, almost without exception. The one exception has been a severe case of 'Yuppie 'Flu' where the client felt worse after exercise. Other clients with less severe 'Yuppie 'Flu' have reported feeling better with gentle walking. Exercise is detrimental, however, during - and for two weeks after - a cold or influenza virus. Certain exercises are contra-indicated with certain medical complaints. *Once again, please contact your medical doctor for the 'go ahead' before starting any form of regular exercise.*

Clients who are depressed frequently tell me that they feel too unmotivated and too tired to exercise. It is too much effort to walk, swim, cycle and so on. Even the thought of exerting themselves is exhausting. I explain that they should not wait to feel more motivated or less tired before exercising. They need to start exercising, and after about two to three weeks they will feel more motivated and less tired and will feel more energised to cope with other demands of daily life.

Close associates
One of the major difficulties facing the person close to a depressed person is that they expend enormous energy trying to 'fix' the depressed person. I hear:

- 'He must start exercising again.'
- 'She needs to tell her boss to go to hell!'

- 'He must learn to relax more.'
- 'He should stop drinking.'
- 'I have tried to explain to her that she has so much for which to be grateful.'

I always ask these clients about caring for themselves, including the role of exercise in their lives. They often do not have time for exercise as they are so busy 'caretaking' the depressed person.

Sara told me that she could not exercise after work because Rob needed supper and she needed to cook for him. I suggested that she took two evenings off a week and one period over the weekend to leave the house and exercise. I also suggested that she give Rob responsibility for cooking or getting take-aways on these weekday evenings. He was happy with the idea of Sara looking after herself, as he felt guilty when he realised the strain his depression was placing on her.

Sara arrived for our appointment the following week with a huge smile on her face. She related the story of Rob's culinary expertise: 'He made spaghetti - lukewarm and stuck together. The mince was in chunks - also not hot. There was a tiny bit of grated cheese on top. I never said a word about the less-than-delicious meal. I saw his face, so proud and self-satisfied at his achievement.' Rob had never before cooked a meal. He enjoyed himself so much that he is reading recipe books and experimenting with other rather exotic meals!

Sara explained that the exercise, per se, was clearing her head, and it gave her time out of the house and away from work. The benefits for her were that she was firming her body, burning up stress, lifting depression and having time-out from cooking the evening meal a few times a week.

The therapist

I am a physically lazy person. Please don't ask me to go on hikes or climb mountains or run marathons. I am, however, convinced of the benefits of regular exercise. For me, this means running on a treadmill or sitting on a stationery bicycle at the gym most mornings. It clears my head and makes me feel physically and emotionally strong. I notice the difference when, for some reason, I have not been able to exercise for 10 days or longer. At these times I feel more stressed and fatigued; problems that I normally cope with seem insurmountable.

Depressed clients and those close to them who have embarked on a regular exercise program, look different:

- Their eyes are brighter.
- They have a bounce in their step.
- They are less anxious and cope better with life's demands and crises.
- They speak about themselves, others and the future in a more positive way.
- They are more motivated and goal directed.

What kind of exercise works?
It seems that non-stop (aerobic-style) exercise is the most beneficial in alleviating symptoms of depression and stress. This kind of exercise includes:

- walking
- jogging/running
- dancing
- swimming
- cycling

It is important to choose one or a combination of aerobic-style exercises that appeals to you and does not bore you. It is important to choose exercise that is going to be easily available. For example, if you like swimming, do you have your own swimming pool, or is there one close to your home or work? Are you able to swim in the cold winter months? Is there an indoor, heated pool that you are able to use on a regular basis? It might help time to pass if you listen to music, read or watch television whilst you exercise on a stationary bicycle. You might prefer to run or walk with a friend. This gives you companionship and a commitment to specific times.

Be sure to stop exercising during and for about two weeks after suffering from a cold or influenza virus and/or other infections. Consult with your doctor before restarting your exercise program.

How often should you exercise?
You should aim to exercise three to four times a week. It is a good idea to exercise on alternate days of the week. It appears that the beneficial effects of exercise spill over onto the days when you are not exercising.

For how long should you exercise?
Each exercise period should last for 20 to 30 minutes. I have experienced and have observed my clients feeling more relaxed and more resistant to stress immediately after exercise, with some carry-over effect into the following day. After three weeks to a month of regular aerobic-style exercise, the antidepressant benefit seems to come into effect.

What do the fitness experts say?
In view of the positive results that I have seen with exercise and depression, I contacted a leading fitness expert in Cape Town, Professor Tim Noakes (Author of *Lore of Running*, 1992). I wanted to know if certain antidepressant and/or tranquillising chemicals are released in the exercising person's body. Prof. Noakes told me that there are hypotheses that these chemicals are produced, but no scientific research has proven that fact. He, however, has stated in his book that jogging, together with antidepressant medication, are beneficial in the treatment of depression[1]. Research has shown that the majority of moderately fit people described themselves as 'very happy'[2]. It has also been found that people who were physically fit from exercise training were less anxious than those who did not exercise[3]. Research studies suggest that symptoms of depression decrease with higher levels of fitness from exercise[4].

Summary
I have been looking at exercise from a broad perspective: that of the depressed client, those close to the depressed person and the therapist. As I am not an expert in the area of fitness, I have provided some insights from experts in this field as well as the results of research that has been conducted. I conclude with the same thought with which I started this section:

Exercise works!

DEEP MUSCLE RELAXATION WITH CREATIVE VISUALISATION AND MUSIC

As you are aware, depression and stress are close companions. You, who are close to a depressed person, also experience anxiety by association. I, too, need to remain calm in my interaction with you and others.

Another most effective manner of handling the stress associated with depression is deep muscle relaxation with creative visualisation and music. I have recorded this relaxation process onto audio-tape. There is an order form at the back of this book should you wish to purchase the tape.

If you do not have the tape read the following instructions onto a blank audio cassette and then play it back to yourself:

Effective stress management utilises left-brain function (the conscious, critical, analytical, logical and intellectual faculties: studying a new language, problem-solving, learning to make art, learning to play a musical instrument).

There is also a focus on the right-brain functioning (the subconscious, intuitive, perceptual and sensory faculties: listening to music, appreciating the beauty of nature, responding to intuition in making decisions).

Deep muscle relaxation is one of the most effective and least time-consuming methods of stress management. This technique will be used with creative visualisation. During this exercise, the left brain (or conscious mind) will be put into 'neutral' and left to rest. The right brain (or subconscious mind) will be focused and stimulated. Your only task will be to allow the power of your subconscious mind to control your body. Your muscles will relax and the use of your senses (in creative visualisation) will further enhance your sense of relaxation.

Sit comfortably on your chair. Loosen any clothing that might be tight. You may change your position at any time, and this will not disturb your sense of peace and calmness. You will be fully aware of my voice and any noise around you. I am going to ask you to systematically tense and relax all the muscle systems in your body. If any of your muscles are injured or painful, do not tense these.

Tense your fists, tight and hard as you can... bend your arms up to make your biceps tight... move your elbows towards each other, so that you feel the muscles pulling across your back... suck your stomach in... don't forget to breathe... press down with your heels and lift your toes up to tense the muscles in your legs... close your eyes tight, clench your teeth and press your lips together... bend your head backwards to make the muscles in the front of your neck tight... breathe through your nose... if your nose is blocked, open your mouth to breathe...

Feel the tightness and tension throughout your body... now let it go... take a deep breath and allow your muscles to relax... continue to breathe deeply and rhythmically... each time you breathe in, feel yourself breathing in peace... as you breathe out, feel tensions draining out of your body through imaginary holes at the bottom of your feet... keep your eyes closed, as I once again ask you to tense the muscles, as I name them, and then release the tension to demonstrate the difference between a state of extreme physical stress and relaxed peacefulness...

Tense your fists, your biceps, your stomach, your legs, your eyes, your teeth, your jaws, your neck... now let them go... take a deep breath and let yourself relax deeper and deeper... let your breathing continue to be deep and rhythmical...

As you sit there with your eyes closed, I am going to count backwards from three to one... as I do so, you will feel yourself getting lighter and lighter until, at one, you open your eyes, let them close again, and allow yourself to go deeper and deeper, and more relaxed than you are now... three... two... one... you can now open your eyes, let them close and go deeper, more peaceful and relaxed... your breathing deep and rhythmical... each time you breathe in, you breathe in calm and peace, as you breathe out, any tension left in your body flows out the bottom of your feet.

Sitting calm, relaxed and peaceful, I want you to imagine a place or scene that you have visited, where you have felt completely relaxed. If you have not experienced such a place, make one up... put yourself into that scene in your mind and get in touch with all the sensations you associate with it... see the colours and shapes that are there... feel the textures that surround you... feel the temperature... hear the sounds... smell the odours... and taste the tastes... take a deep breath and go deeper... peaceful, calm and relaxed... your breathing is deep and rhythmical...

I am once again going to count backwards from three to one, suggesting lightness with each count... you may find that your subconscious mind wishes you to go deeper and deeper with my counting, rather than lighter and lighter... it does not matter which, but at one you will open your eyes, allow them to close again and go deeper than you are now... three... two... one... open your eyes, let them close and go deeper... peaceful and relaxed... I now want you to imagine there is a soothing liquid inside your head... let it be a colour and a temperature that you find relaxing ... let the liquid move inside your head... slowly, gently *massaging the muscles... leaving them limp, heavy and relaxed... feel the liquid move into your neck... soothing, healing and relaxing the muscles... into your shoulders... dissolving any tensions that might still be there... into your arms... relaxing the muscles and leaving them heavy and limp... into your back muscles... massaging, healing and soothing... into your chest... relaxing the muscles... into your hip and pelvic area, relaxing and soothing the muscles... into your legs, dissolving any tensions that might still be there... feel the liquid flow into your feet, massaging the muscles and releasing tensions... now feel the liquid flow out through the imaginary holes at the bottom of your feet... take a deep breath and as you breathe out go deeper... peaceful, calm and relaxed...*

I am now going to count backwards slowly from five to one... suggesting lightness as I do so. Whether you go deeper and deeper or lighter and lighter with my counting will depend on the wishes of your subconscious mind... at one you will be able to open your eyes, you will feel refreshed, as if you have had a long holiday... you will feel alert with a deep sense of peace and inner confidence... you will know the power that your mind has over your body... five... four... three... two... one... you can open your eyes.

Relaxation occurs faster and more deeply the second time you practise the technique. It then follows that the more frequently the method is practised, the less time it takes to achieve deep muscle relaxation and the more efficient and effective it will be.

Also, the use of relaxation techniques from your own experience will provide a personalised combination that is well balanced, varied and particularly suited to your own lifestyle. It may, for example, be useful to play music cassettes in the car to combat the stress of heavy traffic. You may choose to relax at home in a warm bath (with or without music) or to go out into the garden and relax with nature, again with or without music.

Now let your eyes close... concentrate on your breathing and you will find that with each breath out you relax deeper and deeper... count backwards from three to one a few times... each time you reach one, open your eyes... let them close and become more fully relaxed than before... three... two... one... open your eyes... let them close and relax deeper... three... two... one... open your eyes... let them close and go deeper... with your mind and body relaxed, feel the soothing liquid flow through your body, take yourself to your peaceful scene in your mind... hear the music and watch the reflected patterns the light makes on your eyes... feel the effects of the music broadening and enriching your sense of calm.

Slowly count backwards from five to one... you will gradually feel yourself becoming lighter and lighter... or deeper or deeper... whichever your subconscious mind decides... at one you will be able to open your eyes feeling refreshed, peaceful, calm, and relaxed five... four... three ... two... one... open your eyes.

Steps to deep muscle relaxation

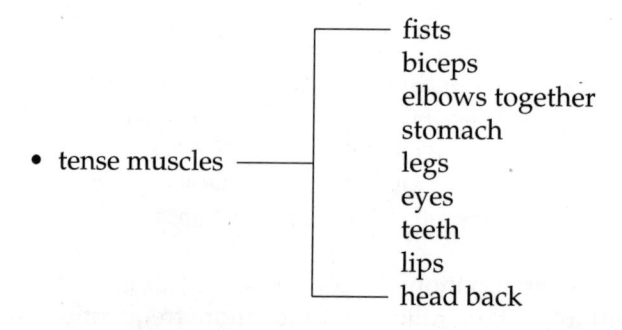

- tense muscles
  - fists
  - biceps
  - elbows together
  - stomach
  - legs
  - eyes
  - teeth
  - lips
  - head back

- relax muscles
- deep breathing
- counting backwards from three to one
- special place - breathing in sensations
- counting backwards from three to one
- liquid flowing
- counting backwards from five to one

The depressed client
Jenny described the effects of deep muscle relaxation: 'As you know, I was so agitated that I could not concentrate. I started exercising regularly and this made me feel much calmer. I then used your relaxation tape at the end of the day. It was wonderful. I felt soothed and relaxed and could fall asleep like a baby.'

Close associates
Gina explained to me how the relaxation exercises made her difficult path much easier. She said, 'I was terrified of Nick's

reaction to my leaving him. I knew that I had to remain calm if I was going to make this monumental leap. Having your tape with me was like having you with me. Your voice was soothing to my soul. I relaxed more than I have ever relaxed before. My muscles were limp and I felt a deep sense of peace and tranquillity. It felt as if I were fortifying myself to walk through the fire.'

The therapist
It was during my training as a psychologist that I started to develop this deep muscle relaxation process. It evolved from an understanding of and the modified use of Jacobson's progressive muscle relaxation. His method is used for desensitising clients to fears and phobias. Also, my supervisor during my Master's and Doctoral studies, Prof. David Fourie, had completed his Doctoral studies on hypnotherapy. I am privileged to have had a six-year apprenticeship in the principles and practice of hypnotherapy. Deep muscle relaxation is a basis for hypnotic suggestion. The relaxed client is more open to suggestion. The modification and integration of Jacobson's and Fourie's methods with my own, together with creative visualisation and the addition of music has proved to be effective as a base for both hypnosis and managing stress. When used for the management of stress, the suggestions that I give to the client are for further peace, calm, confidence and relaxation. My clients generally report that they have never before experienced such a deep sense of calm.

I have observed enormous therapeutic benefits from inducing relaxation in those of my clients who are stressed and depressed and those who are close to a stressed and depressed person. Also, in order to manage my own stress from working with troubled clients, I use this method myself between seeing clients. As a client leaves my rooms I visualise them flowing out of the bottom of my feet. I then breathe in peacefulness before letting the next client into my rooms. This helps me to heal and restores my resources to feel strong and calm for each client. I use the longer relaxation process at the end of a working day, before I go out for the evening or before bed. I also find this method helpful when I wake up in the morning. This method has been discussed in detail in my book, *Stress Matters*.

Summary

This section has provided a practical method of managing stress for the depressed client, for those close to the depressed person and for me, the therapist. Deep muscle relaxation with creative visualisation is, in fact, a technique that benefits everyone. It is an effective way of 'pausing' regularly in our hectic lives, in order to feed, heal and replenish ourselves for more efficient and effective functioning at home and at work.

SAYING NO – 'GUT'-STUFF

You have now incorporated the concepts of exercise and deep muscle relaxation into your life. Add to these the ability to listen carefully and respond to your 'gut', in refusing unreasonable or manipulative requests. You will then have a powerful repertoire of skills for managing depression and for coping with a close association with a depressed person. My research and clinical experience with depression points to the following:

- Depressed clients do not generally trust their 'gut' instincts, and will frequently say 'Yes' rather than 'No' in response to unreasonable or manipulative requests.
- Those close to a depressed person will often report that they 'give in' to the depressed person's demands because they feel sorry for him or her.

In both these situations, the person unable to say 'No' is left feeling resentful, frustrated, angry and depressed. If you don't know about 'gut feel', try the following:

The next time you speak to someone (preferably someone you know, so that you can explain afterwards what you were doing), stand closer to them than is usually comfortable for you. Maintain eye-contact with the person and then move even closer. You will feel anxious or uncomfortable somewhere in the region of your solar plexus. When you feel this kind of discomfort in your gut, you should be saying 'No' rather than 'Yes', to unreasonable or manipulative requests. It is especially important to say 'No' when your gut continues to feel uncomfortable for any length of time. That is 'GUT STUFF'! Your gut will feel comfortable when you need to say 'Yes' to a request. 'Gut stuff' is the basis for a book on its own, because it also involves the handling of criticism and making important life decisions. I am, however, going to focus on *saying* 'No' for the purpose of managing depression.

Manuel Smith[5] suggests that we think of a situation where someone at work or at home is demanding time or material gain from us. Our gut reaction to this request is clearly uncomfortable. The person is trying to make us agree by inducing guilt feelings. In this type of situation, we express empathy/understanding of the person's need, but then say 'No' with no explanation, defence, aggression or withdrawal.

The depressed client
Rob seemed to have hit the depths of depression when he felt pressured to accept promotion in an area of work with which he did not feel comfortable. He was uncomfortable with the promotion but, being anxious to please, he rationalised his discomfort. Later, having expressed his discomfort to his superiors, he was moved into an area of work that he wanted and enjoys. Rob is no longer depressed. Rob's saying 'No' was not the miracle 'cure' for his severe depression, but it certainly had a markedly positive effect on his mood.

Jenny also felt far less depressed when she refused to orchestrate her life around her mother's alcoholic binges.

Close associates
Gina described how saying 'No' to a destructive relationship helped her increasingly to trust her 'gut' (instinctual) feelings and to act on these: 'Nick used to tell me that my feelings were wrong and that I was over-sensitive. After many years of believing him, rather than my "gut", I started to listen and trust myself. To act on these "gut" feelings was the hard part but, with practice, I have become quite good at it. Now I find that whenever I listen to and act on my "gut" feelings, I feel brave, confident, happier and more positive about myself and my life. There are times, however, when I hear my gut saying, "No!" but I consciously decide to accede to the person's request. The cost in terms of time and effort to say "No" is not always worth it. In these situations I do not feel bad, because I am conscious of what I am doing and why. I like to understand my "gut" feelings as a sort of spiritual guide. There must be a connection to forces greater than I am because they are always spot on, even when I cannot, at the time, find any logical

reason why I feel discomfort. The rational reason becomes clear at some later time.'

The therapist
One of my strongest tools in therapeutic interaction with clients is my 'gut' feel. I find that, when I gather information by asking questions and more questions, and when I recognise the responses to these (both verbal and non-verbal) and then listen to my 'gut', I am connecting my head with my heart and can work quickly and effectively. My clients seem to improve and develop at a much faster rate when I am in tune with my 'gut' feelings. At the same time, I encourage my clients to get in touch with their own 'gut' feelings. I encourage them to listen to and explore these feelings and to act on them in their own time. I also promote the idea of gathering and investigating factual information about the matter on hand.

Sometimes it happens that a client's 'gut' feeling is obvious to me. My client is relating situations where he or she felt depressed and anxious and I can see quite clearly that this is because the client is going against strong 'gut' feel.

Take the case of Angela, 41, an unmarried, pregnant client, most of whose family and friends had suggested that she abort her baby. Her mother had been horrified when told of the pregnancy and begged Angela to have an abortion because she felt that she would never be able to face the neighbours if she were to have an illegitimate grandchild. The father of Angela's child had also urged her to have an abortion because he never had any intention of leaving his wife with whom he already had a young family.

Angela knew that by refusing to consider abortion, she would lose her lover and, temporarily, the support of her mother. She realised that, because she was pregnant, her job opportunities would be limited, but that she would have to find a job at which she could work half-days so that she would have some means of support once her baby was born.

In therapy with me, Angela raised several topics that were worrying her such as whether she would ever be able to find a man who would want her, pregnant now, and later with a small child.

During a few sessions, I questioned, listened and observed. Then I questioned and listened some more. I could see and hear, very quickly, that Angela was going to keep her baby despite all opposition. She was frightened of the difficulties that would follow her decision, but her 'gut' feeling was very strong that she would keep her baby anyway. I needed to hold back my own comments for a while so that she could clarify her own thoughts and feelings. I also needed to examine very carefully the things I thought I was seeing (her 'gut' feeling). I had to understand whether what I was seeing and feeling and hearing had anything to do with my own wish to have a baby, or any negative feelings that I might have about abortion. Once I had clarified these points and was sure that I was not going to influence Angela's decision with my own issues, I told her that I could see and hear that her 'gut' feel was to say 'No' to the abortion requests and 'Yes' to the baby.

This was the first time that Angela had responded to her 'gut' feelings and acted accordingly. She had previously taken decisions that would please others. Once Angela was no longer depressed, I told her that if she listened to her 'gut' in this way for the rest of her life, and acted on it, she would continue to grow in self-confidence and psychological well-being. If she does so, she will not experience depression associated with saying 'Yes' when her gut says 'No' again.

Those people close to a depressed person often tell me how difficult it is to refuse their unreasonable/manipulative demands. This is because of feelings of sympathy, mixed with frustration and guilt, and not being able to help the depressed person to get better. When close associates say 'Yes' instead of 'No', the depressed person frequently becomes more dependent, more demanding and less willing to take responsibility for his or her life. In this way they are therefore keeping the depressed person stuck in his or her depression. The demands are often for close associates to do something or speak to someone on behalf of the depressed person. My late father used to say, 'If there is a mug to carry you, why should you walk?' So the depressed person will remain in a 'patient' role (passive, dependent and depressed).

When close associates stand back and refuse to comply with the unreasonable or manipulative demands of the depressed person, the latter is forced to act for himself or herself and to risk an active rather than passive behavioural style. This active, 'taking of responsibility' elevates the depressed person to one who is more confident and less 'sick'. Also, by removing the label of 'depressed' (therefore 'sick'), close associates are treating the depressed person as an equal, with respect. This shift contradicts the usual pattern of behaviour of a depressed person in relation to those close to him or her.

Close associates will find that they are free from the life-and-death responsibility for the cure for depression. This will release their focus and energy for other, more constructive pursuits.

Summary
This has been a difficult section to write. It is not an easy task to explain 'gut' feeling in a concrete, simple manner. It is, however, a most valuable tool for those who are depressed, for those close to a depressed person, for the therapist and, in fact, for anyone who has choices to make.

CREATIVITY

Regular exercise, relaxation and honing the instinct to act on your 'gut' responses is, hopefully, now integrated into your lifestyle. At worst, you are planning to include these because now that you have learned the benefits, they make sense to you. The expression of creativity forms an essential addition to the self-help methods described above. Creative expression includes:

- making art, pottery or sculpture
- writing
- playing a musical instrument
- singing
- directing, producing and/or acting
- designing clothes
- sewing and/or knitting
- cooking
- designing interiors and/or decorating
- landscape gardening

By utilising your creativity you, the reader, are expressing feelings that are so deep-seated that they defy verbal expression. When my clients use creativity as an integral and regular part of the management of depression, or as a way of coping with someone who is depressed and close to them, the healing process is significantly accelerated.

When you followed the instructions in Part 1 of this book, you were expressing your creativity by:

- storytelling
- creating a collage
- clay modelling

These, and the other forms of creative expression, will leave you feeling tired – sometimes exhausted – as if you have run an emotional marathon. You will feel calmer, but you will also experience a sense of vulnerability. It feels as if you no longer have a protective membrane around your emotions. You might feel quite sad and/or angry. The experience makes you feel like that of a defenceless baby or young child.

Your openness to your feelings is psychologically healthy, but you need your own special brand of nurturing to care for yourself. Imagine that you are the loving care-giver of your own small baby or child. Do those things, for yourself, that you know will heal and soothe the pain of your own 'inner child'. These include:

- eating healthy, nourishing food
- having aromatherapy (more will be said about this later in this book)
- exercising
- relaxing
- treating yourself to something special (material or otherwise)
- enjoying the soothing qualities of nature
- listening to beautiful music
- being with one or more special people who are kind to you and avoiding those who are harsh or judgmental
- being near to, or in water (which is reminiscent of the womb experience)
- anything that you know is good for you and that makes you feel cared for

The depressed client
Jenny loved cooking. She explained, 'I have loved cooking since I was about five. I've now started catering for parties, weddings and barmitzvahs part-time.'

Her eyes were shining, and I could not detect any depression in her body language or speech. She continued, 'Everyone I speak to is excited about what I'm doing. I have already organised a beautiful 21st party. I have bookings for a wedding and an engagement party. I must admit that I'm tired, but I'm happy.'

Then Daniel, a client who was depressed because his young child was being used by his ex-wife in their post-divorce acrimony, described to me how he was using painting to express his anguish. He said, 'My ex-wife has found my Achille's Heel. I feel so angry, frustrated and hurt when she plays mind-games, using my child. The only thing keeping me sane at the moment is losing myself in painting. I am painting big shapes. The colours are mostly black and red. I am like a person demented when I'm painting, but I sleep like a baby afterwards!'

Close associates
Gina described to me how she had used art to understand her emotions after her marriage. She also expressed her repressed sexuality through painting before she became physically involved with another man.

She said, 'Painting is like an explosion of my sexual volcano. The man I made love with after my marriage got the full thrust of 20 years of undiscovered sexuality. We fell off the bed and found ourselves against the glass sliding doors of his bedroom. What passion I have released! It was wonderful, but both the painting and the passionate love-making have left me feeling more open and vulnerable than I've ever felt before. I know that my openness is important for growth but, oh the pain! I felt like a very young child. I had to take good care of myself, so I found a quiet, beautiful beach where I could allow the sea and warm sand and beauty to heal my soul. I felt that G-d was there looking after me.'

Sara, explained to me that she had started sewing again. She said, 'I sew while listening to soothing classical music. My friends and Rob can't believe the quality of the clothes that I'm creating. Time flies when I'm sewing, and I use a part of me that I had devoted to nursing Rob.'

Using creativity helps those close to a depressed person to redirect energy from the fruitless attempt to 'cure' or rescue or 'caretake' the depressed person to healing and strengthening themselves - a far more beneficial pursuit.

The therapist
I regularly need to release the emotions associated with working with troubled clients. To this end, I design my own and friends' gardens, renovate properties, and then decorate their interiors. I give advice to friends and family who like my artistic style. I write books and I create paintings on canvas.

I have recently been involved in a situation in which several school children were found to be taking drugs. At the same time, a friend committed suicide. I felt an urgent need to paint my painful and confused feelings onto canvas. I bought a huge canvas and found that I was depicting the universe on it. Then I painted many young children. At the end of a few agonising days of painting, I could understand my pain and put it into perspective. I had explored deep feelings of the protective, but fallible, role of mothering – mine and others.

Summary
In this section I have attempted to illustrate the beneficial effects of creativity in the management of depression, for those close to a depressed person, and for myself. Clients often tell me that they are not creative, but everyone is creative. Your work does not have to be pretty or clever. You have created with modelling clay, with storytelling and with collage. Find your own medium. It will help to heal and enrich your life.

RELIGIOUS/SPIRITUAL SUPPORT

Being depressed, or having someone close to you who is depressed, is a lonely, isolating experience. If you had suffered a heart attack or stroke, or were caring for a family member who had cancer, you would be likely to receive support from family, friends, work colleagues and others. With depression comes the experience of embarrassment and stigma. Often one feels a non-entitlement to the understanding or support of others. The depressed person feels guilty about his or her depression. No one can see the wounds, and x-rays show no broken bones. The person close to someone who is depressed feels embarrassed about cancelling social arrangements or sitting through a dinner party with a partner who is withdrawn or irritable. Those close to a depressed person also often feel inadequate when they are unable to effect a 'cure' for the depression.

A religious or spiritual belief system is incredibly healing and balancing for the loneliness and isolation so often associated with depression. Some people find religious peace of mind in ritualised and regular attendance at church, synagogue or mosque services. Others find 'soul food' in nature, either hiking up a mountain, watching the sea or simply enjoying the peace of their own gardens. Still others find spiritual/religious support through listening to their 'gut' guidance or in the expression of their creative talents or listening to beautiful music. Experiencing the artistic creations of others is another profound way to experience the universal forces that are more powerful than the individual. You could use one or a combination of these means to connect with your religious/spiritual support system.

The depressed client
It often happens that a depressed person has lost faith, due to his or her suffering, and feels distanced from a previously strong religious or spiritual base. Sometimes depressed clients tell me that they have been too busy to attend to their spiritual needs, or that they do not feel worthy of help from a Higher Being. Others say that they are agnostic, and have no time for religion. These people are often the scientific, logical, left-brain thinkers who cannot find proof of religious or spiritual forces. Generally, these clients express (at a verbal or non-verbal level), an insatiable hunger for love, affection and intimacy. They experience a bottomless pit and an ache deep inside of themselves. At the same time, they fear or deride the revealing of themselves to the forces of the universe. When they do risk this laying bare, their sense of aching loneliness is generally alleviated and they seem to achieve a peace of mind. They feel that they are not alone.

After months of being stuck in the depths of severe depression, Rob told me that he had been heavily involved in church activities through his school years and until his mid-twenties, after which his work demands took up too much time for him to be able to pursue religious activity.

However, he used to take his mother to visit the grave of his father on a fairly regular basis. He said, 'Last week for the first time, I went on my own to the cemetery. I stood at my father's grave and spoke to him. I cried and apologised for not being able to help him more through his illness and to deal with his fear of death. I felt the presence of my father there and I was once again in touch with my religious being. I left feeling less guilty and calmer. I am going to start going to church again.'

Close associates
Gina explained how faith had given her the courage to risk leaving Nick, and to trust that she would be supported. She said, 'I was faced with huge life decisions that would affect my children and myself. I began to listen and to trust my "gut" feel. I started acting on these feelings. I gained more and more confidence in my "gut" feel and took it to be my personal source of guidance. This helped because I was no longer listening to Nick who was telling me that my beliefs, values and actions were bad. When I listened to, and acted on, my "gut" feel (using my head to gather information too), my decisions always proved to be wise. I no longer felt alone or lonely. On the day that I had planned to leave home, I thought that I had only two suitcases. Because the situation was delicate and somewhat dangerous, I had had no time to buy or borrow a third suitcase. I opened the top cupboard in the study, and there in front of me was my father's old brown leather suitcase. I had forgotten that it existed. It had his initials, strong and clear, on the side facing me. I just smiled. I was being helped in a most practical manner.'

The therapist
Until my last year at high school, I was disinterested in religion. I found that the rituals of Judaism limited my extensive socialising. My father had tried to instil in me a love of tradition by urging me to attend synagogue regularly. My mother was cynical about religion. She had been deserted by her rabbi in a time of need as a young mother, when her own mother was ill.

In my final art examination at high school, I started to paint and it felt as if someone was holding my hand. My painting had been wonderful but, to be honest, I had not been able to take credit for the painting – some greater force was helping. This experience had been a surprise but I was not yet convinced. When my children were very young I had gone to a small, country synagogue. I listened to the ancient chanting. I watched my little boys in that devout atmosphere. Something softened inside of me. My faith and trust in a Higher Being and the forces of the universe have grown from strength to strength ever since.

In my personal and professional life, I have an ongoing 'conversation' with my Maker. I give thanks for the assistance that I am regularly given. Sometimes I ask for guidance and support when I need to make major decisions. I always receive this help.

I frequently find the suffering of my clients awesome. I am sometimes at a loss for words. The appropriate words recede from me. How, for example, can I be of help in healing parents who have lost not one, but two young and healthy children through motor accidents at different times? How can I help when my client, the mother of four adolescents, tells me that her cancer has spread to her liver and her doctors can do no for more her? We spent that session being together, without many words. We both had tears streaming down our faces.

Sometimes I need to make assessments of children with recommendations that will profoundly affect their futures and those of their families. This happens with abused children, custody cases or where parents are unable to care properly for their children. The responsibility is enormous and I always ask for spiritual assistance to remain focused and act in the best interests of the child.

I have reached the conclusion that life's difficulties are, in fact, challenges that are sent to test each individual and to provide opportunities to grow through the process. It helps to listen carefully to 'gut' instincts and to act on these after having gathered factual information. It is also healing to ask for spiritual assistance when necessary.

Summary
This section has explored the benefits of religious and spiritual support in the management of depression. Spirituality combines 'gut' feel with creativity and imparts a peace of mind and 'soul food' that has no substitute. It also allows for a sense of rootedness and a base from which to risk new dimensions of being. With strong faith, nothing in life or about dying is so frightening that it can become debilitating.

POSITIVE THINKING

One of the most prevalent symptoms of depression is negativity. One of the most important goals of therapy is the engendering of positive thinking for the depressed person and for those who are close to him or her. More will be said about positive thinking and depression in the section on psychotherapy – more particularly, cognitive psychotherapy.

The depressed client
One of the most stunning examples of positivity I have experienced in my practice was that of a young man in his early 20s who had consulted with me for stress management and assertiveness training. The area he had focused on was confidence in dating. He did exceptionally well in therapy after a relatively short period of time. His passion was skydiving. About a year after our last session, I received a call from his distraught mother who told me he had completed 400 sky dives, but had been involved in a motor accident on his return home. He was in hospital, a paraplegic. I went to visit him and found him in a critical condition. We talked and he told me that he was going to leave the hospital and challenge the world in his wheel chair. I was speechless (not a common occurrence for me). Scott Peck[6] has stated that life is tough, and that once a person acknowledges that life is difficult and fraught with crises, it becomes more manageable. The acceptance of life's crises is the first step towards positive thinking. It is quite normal to be anxious, distressed and even depressed when we are faced with life's difficulties or crises. Allow yourself a limited period of self-pity, after which it becomes necessary not only to identify the actual problem, but also to decide what action to take to effect change. It is also helpful to look for the positive lessons that inevitably arise from life's crises.

Positive thinking includes a spiritual/religious belief system in which one accepts that each person is sent certain lessons. Free choice involves deciding whether to face these tasks in a positive, constructive manner or whether to avoid life's difficulties and to choose rather to be a victim – miserable, stressed and depressed.

Close associates
Gina described to me how she took negative and dangerous predicaments as challenges and opportunities to dig deep down into her inner resources, to learn and to grow.

She said, 'I had faith that I was not alone in my difficulties. Nick knows that my children are my weakness. He belittled me in front of them. I saw their split loyalties and I felt their pain. I protected them where I could, but there were times when I had no option but to allow them to face great emotional hardships. My message to them was that their difficulties were part of life's lessons. I have also told them that they have choices. They may choose negative behaviours such as drug-taking or blaming me and their father. The better option is to acknowledge their pain, express it, and then learn constructive ways to strengthen and improve their coping skills. In retrospect, I am immensely proud of these young people who are growing into fine, caring human beings. We all wobble from time to time and are allowed a short period of irritability and self-pity. Then we find new and positive ways of dealing with crises. I am sad that Nick is unable to learn from life in the superb way in which his children have done. It is also interesting that he told me that, if I left him, he would make sure that I was destroyed. He said that I would be like a turkey without a head, that he would chop the turkey's head off. He has certainly tried, but all that has happened is that I have become stronger and stronger through learning to cope and survive.'

The therapist
My aim in writing this book is, in fact, a paradox. I wanted to write a positive book on depression – perhaps a contradiction in terms. I hope that you, the reader, will feel hopeful and positive despite your pain. I am not presumptuous enough to ignore or negate your pain and fear. My hope is that you will acknowledge the depth of your distress and use the methods discussed here to empower yourself, to improve the quality of your life and to grow from strength to strength.

I have always attempted to create a therapeutic climate for my depressed clients and those close to them, where they are able to set the pace of growth, which I follow, one step behind. Here, I listen to negativity, hopelessness, despair and suicidal thoughts, but for a limited period. Then we discuss alternative ways of thinking and of planning lifestyle.

My greatest challenge is the depressed client who has had many years of being a 'patient' who is 'sick' – and close associates who have a need to define the depressed person as 'unstable'. I redefine the roles of the depressed client and and close associates in an attempt to put them on a more equal footing. This process involves mutual respect. I also use humour and as much positivity as I am able. If, however, my depressed clients (and/or close associates) remain stuck in their previous roles, I end therapy with the message that it is not yet time for growth. I must emphasise here that growth and change are processes that sometimes take a long time. It happens, for example, that clients think intellectually about change and feel that they are growing (at a 'gut' emotional level), but are not yet ready for action. These patients have made an emotional and/or intellectual shift, and I work happily with them. Also, the life choices that they make are their own. I respect that people may choose to maintain the status quo. Take for example Carly, an alcoholic client whose baby had died. She and I worked together for about six months on connecting 'head/heart' matters, and clarifying the ideals that she wanted from life. One was to stop drinking. When she felt strong and clear, she stopped drinking.

When I do end therapy with 'stuck' clients they know that they are free to contact me again when they do feel ready for change. They have frequently contacted me later, when their readiness for change is obvious. We can then work quickly and effectively and the change of pattern is remarkable. Some 'stuck' clients do not reconnect with me. I understand that we either do not 'fit' as therapist and client, or our timing is not in sync.

Summary
In this section I have tried to show how depression and positive thinking cannot peacefully coexist. Negativity can be a comfortable habit which it is essential to break.

TOUCH – SENSUAL AND SEXUAL

Touch is an interesting concept when related to the management of depression, for the depressed person and those close to him or her. We have already described how a depressed person often feels withdrawn at an emotional and physical level and libido is generally low. At the same time, the depressed person is hungry for emotional and physical closeness and is hurt by his or her isolation and loneliness. Those close to the depressed person receive these double messages (the need and demand for attention together with the rejection, by the depressed person, of any attempt to offer intimate connection). This leaves close associates feeling confused and sometimes frustrated and immobilised. Add to this scenario the other ambivalent feelings of those close to the depressed person – sympathy and irritation. Close associates often feel rejected by the depressed person and are lonely, even though they are in a relationship. There is also the broader social isolation due to the social stigma and embarrassment.

How, then, could I suggest touch as an effective manager for depression? Because it is incredibly healing for both the depressed person and those close to him or her! One reason for this is that the skin is the largest of the sense organs. We have already discussed how stimulation of the senses is highly beneficial as a stress and depression manager. Deep muscle relaxation, with creative visualisation and music focus on the visual, auditory, olfactory, taste and tactile senses.

Sensual touch should involve generous and sensitive helpings of sensual pleasuring of your partner. Listen to what kind of sensual touch your partner wants (how hard, how soft and in which direction). Avoid any pressure to perform sexually. Each partner should have an opportunity to give pleasure and to be pleasured, without pressure. It is helpful to use body lotion or massage oil. Create a relaxing environment using soothing music, soft lighting or candles, aromatherapy oils burning in a lamp and a warm room.

This type of sensual pleasuring requires deep communication of wants and needs. Use 'gut' feel to express comfort and pleasure, or discomfort, when your partner is touching you. Do not hesitate to ask for what you need. It is important that your partner does not take your, 'No!' personally but rather, understands it as your expression of preference at this special time.

Sensual pleasuring, over time, promotes close connection and trust which creates a climate of reassurance. It also heals deep feelings of loneliness and isolation. When trust and emotional intimacy have developed there can be a gradual movement towards sexual touch. Again, maintain honest communication between partners about that which is comfortable and pleasurable, or that which does not feel good. When sexuality has been established, ensure that it generally happens within the context of sensual pleasuring. It should also be mentioned that, from time to time, you may simply feel the need for a fast release of sexual tensions – this too is healthy.

There are other means of sensual touch that fall outside the realm of an emotionally and physically intimate relationship. These include:

- aromatherapy (this will be discussed in the section on holistic treatment of depression)
- reflexology
- hugging friends
- rubbing the backs or feet of your children, or stroking their hair, or letting them do the same for you
- touching and stroking pet dogs and cats
- walking barefoot on soft grass or sand

The depressed client
Jenny told me about her past experiences with touch. She said, 'I can never remember receiving a hug from my parents. The only time they touched me was to hit me. I hugged my brother a lot and that was soothing for me. I thought that if I was very good, my parents would hug and kiss me, but I think that they were so caught up in their lives that they didn't even think about touching us kindly. When I got married, my husband touched me in a sexual way, but would not otherwise hold my hand or show me any affection. Some time after my divorce I met a man who touched me so gently – from kisses and strokes of my head and face to each of my fingers and toes. This left me feeling open and vulnerable but so very satisfied. I cried like a baby from the wonderful feeling of it and from the sadness of what I had been missing all my life until then. I got so much pleasure from his touch and he showed me how to touch him. Being a giving kind of person, I seemed to get as much pleasure from his enjoyment of my touching him.'

Close associates
Sara described how touch had helped her and Rob to feel better. She said, 'When Rob was going through his depressed phases he would not touch me. I felt so lonely that I would sometimes watch him sleeping, and cry from loneliness. I decided to start to touch him again. I first touched his arm when we passed in the passage. I then stroked his head a bit and, when he didn't protest, I sat between his legs and he started to stroke my hair – it was so reassuring. We touched each other a lot and, after a long time, we were on the floor, kissing and hugging and undressing each other.

We made passionate love for the first time in months. We both decided that this touching "thing" felt so good we were going to do it again, even if he felt depressed.'

The therapist
You will probably have noticed, from the tone of this section, that I am convinced of the benefits of touch. Touch conjures up images of indulgence, pampering, pleasure, relaxation, passion and luxury. When touch is not yet a part of my clients' repertoire, I am generally able to convince them of the benefits. Sometimes it takes a while for depressed clients, and those close to them, to take the first step towards touching. When they do, they report feelings of relaxation and wellbeing and, should they be in relationships, they talk of greater emotional and physical intimacy.

Summary
This section has been an attempt to describe how sensual and sexual touch stimulates the largest sense organ, the skin. Touch is also an effective way of overcoming the loneliness and isolation associated with depression.

SPACE

In the section on *touch* I have encouraged the promotion of physical and emotional intimacy as healing factors in depressed systems. This closeness implies the opposite of withdrawal (a common symptom associated with depression). Why, then, do I also suggest 'space' to manage depression?

The 'space' part of this prescription involves listening to your 'gut' when you need time to be alone. Drop the associated guilt and redefine your space as a positive basic need. Use phrases like 'chilling out', 'time to smell the roses', 'space for replenishment', 'spiritual connection' and 'psychological holiday from the demands of daily living'. Associate your space with pleasure, healing and nourishment.

If you are suffering from depression, you will probably find that those around you become anxious and mildly critical if you express the need to be alone. If you are close to a depressed person, you might feel guilty about taking time for your own needs.

For all concerned, I suggest a balance between periods of close, interpersonal connection and periods of space.

The ways in which you create space are unique to your own desires. Below are some suggestions:

- Unplug the telephone.
- Climb a mountain.
- Take a nature hike.
- Watch a movie in the middle of the day.
- Walk or sit next to the sea, a lake or river.
- Go river rafting.
- 'Sloth' for a whole day: not shaving, if you are a man, staying in bed late, feeling indulgent, not guilty.
- Take a long bath or shower.
- Switch off the lights and light candles while you daydream or meditate.
- Go window shopping on your own.
- Sit in a crowded coffee shop where you do not know anyone and enjoy watching the people.

You will know that you are 'taking healing space' when you feel a delicious, decadent kind of truancy – definitely without guilt. You will want to 'Ooh!' and 'Aah!' about your space.

The depressed client
Rob told me that he had always been a person who needed a lot of space. He said, 'I serve people the whole day, so I love the quiet of home. Give me music or television, and I am able to switch off and get my sanity back. Sara knows when I am in my own space. She says that I'm "not there". She has learnt to leave me alone at those times. This does not mean that I am depressed, just in a quiet place. I don't even need to be on my own to take space. I can just switch off. It is as necessary for me as food.'

Close associates
Sara finds her space in sewing or going to the gym. She said, 'I have stopped feeling guilty about taking space. It feels wonderful and well-deserved.'

James, who is married to Carly, explains, 'I take my space by doing something physical and mechanical. I paint the house or fix the woodwork, or I make something. It allows me "time out" in my head and, at the same time, I feel that I have achieved something.'

The therapist
For me, space is essential, especially as I engage in intense conversation with clients on a daily basis. I am immensely satisfied by this work but believe that I will not be as effective if I do not lighten up and take space after hours. I divide my time away from work between enjoyment of family and close friends and time on my own. When my house is empty, I sometimes switch my classical music on loud and lose myself in the brilliant creativity of others. I might have a long, luxurious bath, with aromatherapy oils and candle-light, or spend time feeding and watering my lush tropical garden. I listen to what I need in terms of space at any particular time and try to do what I need. Today, for example, is Sunday. My house has been taken over by teenage children who are sleeping late after their Saturday night out. I have left them to wake and have breakfast at their leisure. I am sitting in a crowded coffee shop, writing this book. The people here do not bother me. In fact, they allow me space to write without feeling lonely.

My clients who are depressed, or who are close to someone who is depressed, do not take long to get in touch with their need for space. They are also quickly able to associate space with wellbeing and health, and to dissociate space from guilt and selfishness.

Summary
In this section, I have encouraged you to take regular periods of space for positive healing as a necessity in the management of depression, just like the other forms of soul food that we have discussed thus far.

HUMOUR

By its very nature, depression is a miserable state to be in. Also, as I mentioned earlier, this misery is contagious to those close to a depressed person. A sense of humour is, therefore, far removed from a depressed system. It is also a helpful way of lightening the tense, negative atmosphere that surrounds a depressed person and those close to him or her.

The depressed client
Rob smiled at me weakly for the first time when he described the antics of his new, mischievous puppy. Towards the end of therapy, Rob related to me an incident in which he refused an unreasonable request from a particularly obnoxious superior and had not worried about whether or not he would receive approval. Rob imitated his boss's facial expression and we both burst out laughing. I knew then that he was near the end of therapy.

Close associates
Gina descibed the humorous aspects of her terrifying and dangerous departure from her marriage. She said, 'My closest friend delivered a note to Nick after I had left. She left her car ignition on for a speedy getaway. She crept up the driveway, in the dark, and, as she was bending down on all fours to push the note under the door, she imagined Nick opening the door to find her, on hands and knees, caught in the act! I believe seeing the funny side to my predicament was an important element to my survival.'

The therapist
I share a waiting room with physiotherapists and speech therapists who treat young children. The children's parents come, week after week, and wait while their children are having treatment. A mother once remonstrated with me because she saw me laughing with a couple as I saw them to the door. She told me that therapy should be serious, 'so why were we laughing?' I too need humour in order to survive in my profession, in the course of which I listen to so much of my clients' pain.

Summary
In this section I have shown that the promotion of humour is healing for depressed clients and those close to them. It is also a vital tool for me as a therapist.

NUTRITION

We have, so far, talked about the non-edible feeding (of the soul) in the management of depression: spiritual and religious feeding, space, touch, relaxation with creative visualisation and music, and humour. While soul-food is important for everyone involved with depression, so are the concepts of physical appetite: increased or decreased desire for food and nutrition.

Medical doctors, psychiatrists and psychologists always question the depressed client about any changes in his or her appetite. These changes, together with sleep disturbances (too much, too little or early waking), are strong indicators of depression.

As a depressed person will probably feel fatigued and sorely lacking in energy, it is important to avoid foods that are high in sugars and fats as these will give you a quick lift followed by a 'let down' in energy as the blood sugar level drops. It is better to follow a diet rich in fresh fruit and vegetables, complex carbohydrates (whole wheat bread, brown rice) and protein in the form of fish and poultry or legumes, with nuts and soya for vegetarians. Less emphasis should be placed on red meat to avoid the heavy, full feeling that often follows the consumption of red meat. A doctor and/or dietician should be consulted for a more individualised eating programme.

You may also consult your doctor or pharmacist for vitamin supplements which address the stress and fatigue associated with depression. The supplements that are recommended are rich in vitamins B and C and calcium. These are generally available without a doctor's prescription. There are, however, certain multivitamins that may only be obtained with a doctor's prescription. One that is used quite extensively and effectively for dealing with depression and stress in South Africa, is Gericomplex®. This has a high percentage of the necessary vitamins, including the B complex, and contains a stimulant.

Together with a healthy diet and vitamin supplements, a depressed person should consider the addition of magnesium to his or her daily nutritional intake. Slow-Mag®, for example, is a compound of highly concentrated magnesium that is available both in tablet and effervescent form. Magnesium appears to take the edge off anxiety and aids in the lifting of depression. It also prevents the craving for sweet things. Dolomite is a natural remedy that also has a fairly high concentration of magnesium, together with calcium.

The depressed client
Carly had stopped drinking alcohol. She no longer had an escape route from her pain through drinking and so was struggling with the reality of depressive symptoms. She told me that she had previously binged to bursting point and had put on a lot of weight during earlier episodes of depression. This time, however, she was so tired that she had not been able to eat anything solid for 10 days. She had been feeling dizzy and had fainted the day before. She had been drinking small amounts of water, but this was obviously not sufficient to prevent dehydration. Her inability to eat had also contributed significantly to her feeling tired, weak and unmotivated. She had lost an enormous amount of weight during the past 10 days.

It was essential for Carly, the psychiatrist and myself to address her nutritional needs urgently. She did not wish to be hospitalised. We decided that she would be able to manage small amounts of a highly nutritional liquid supplement at regular intervals throughout the day. She also needed to drink more water to avoid dehydration. She was advised to consume this nutritional liquid and water at her own pace. She was to start introducing small helpings of solid food once a day after a week. Within a month, she was able to eat small, regular and healthy meals, spaced throughout the day. She was including a multivitamin and magnesium supplement daily. She reported that she was feeling stronger.

Close associates
I have described how those close to a depressed person often 'catch' the depression. If this should be the case with you, follow the nutritional advice above. Should you be feeling stressed and tired from your close association with a depressed person, the nutritional guidelines will be of benefit to you, too. Whilst you may suggest nutritionally healthy eating patterns to the depressed person, you do not need to cajole him or her to eat. Leave that responsibility to the professionals and to the depressed person, otherwise you will be taking on the role of 'caretaker'. This role will keep the depressed person 'sick'. What one can do is understand that the depressed person's energy level is low and that he or she may need to eat slowly, or small amounts. One may also wish to help with, or do, the shopping for the necessary foods

and supplements. Should the depressed person be so tired as to be unable to eat or drink, his or her doctor, psychiatrist or psychologist might consider hospitalisation.

The therapist
I always ask the depressed person and those close to him or her about their appetites and eating patterns. It has been my experience that clients who feel mildly depressed frequently binge uncontrollably, especially on junk food. These clients put on weight which makes them feel more depressed. Clients who are severely depressed often experience a marked decrease in appetite with corresponding weight loss. Another observation is that when a client is depressed due to intense love relationship matters, he or she often loses a lot of weight. I do not worry in these cases as their appetites and weights normalise with time.

Summary
In this section, I have shown how changes in appetite and eating patterns are fundamental to the experience of depression. These disturbances are also frequently experienced by those depressed and/or stressed on account of being closely involved with a depressed person.

Remember, whether you are the depressed person or someone close, take care of the nutritional needs of your body. If you are the person close to someone who is depressed, be caring towards that person. Also, show respect for their wishes. Be careful not to take the 'caretaker' role as this will keep the depressed person 'sick', dependent and feeling inferior in relation to you.

FINANCIAL MANAGEMENT

Depressed people and those close to them often feel insecure and out of control. Their financial affairs (losses or in chaos) are frequently triggers for depression.

Facing the financial 'monsters' is the first step towards regaining a sense of control. It is neither how much nor how little your income is that is important, but rather how to spend less than you earn, and how to reduce debts that will improve your sense of wellbeing.

It is also helpful to examine the symbolic meanings that you place on finance, and the ways in which the family in which you were raised handled and thought about money. You will probably find that you are following your parents' patterns or doing the opposite. Examine whether your ways of handling your finances, whatever the origins, are constructive or destructive.

Should your financial affairs be complicated, it would be advisable to call on the assistance of a financial planning expert. This may cost you money but it could save you a lot in the long term.

The depressed client
Jenny said, 'Part of the reason for my depression was the guilt that I felt about not curing my parents' alcohol addictions. In retrospect, another big trigger was the financial noose I put around my neck when I bought my beach-front apartment. On the one hand, it was important for me to own my own property. On the other hand, I bought an apartment that would have been big enough for my mother, had she chosen to come and live with me. I could have taken care of her and prevented her from drinking. Unfortunately, the monthly repayments took practically my whole salary. Also, my mother was not interested in coming to live with me. At this stage I've realised that I cannot stop her drinking. The other thing that I've come to realise is that my insecurity about money, and my need to own expensive property, stems from my need to avoid my parents' poverty-stricken lifestyle. Their problems with money were, however, alcohol-related - mine aren't. After speaking to you and to a financial advisor, I have decided to keep my apartment. I am doing well from my after-hours catering business and have asserted myself at work by asking for and receiving an increase in salary. My present income now covers my mortgage bond, with money over for living expenses. I am even able to treat myself to a luxury from time to time. I am not rich, but I have enough to be able to sleep peacefully at night. With this sense of financial control, together with the resolution of old family conflicts, my confidence has increased and my depression has lifted'.

Close associates
Gina described the meaning that money has for her. She said, 'Nick kept telling me that his bad moods would go away when he was

rich. He used to tell me that I was responsible for his financial support. Remember, he had married a financial investment. I used to feel so incredibly insecure and humiliated when he overspent and his cheques bounced. My embarrassment and insecurity worsened when he deposited his cheques into my account. His cheques bounced and then my cheques bounced due to insufficient funds in my account. He could never understand my insecurity and humiliation. I used to try to explain that it was to do with honesty and values. Both his parents and mine had lived within their means, and that was how I wanted to live. For a while, after I left Nick, I was painfully cautious with my finances. Then I went through a phase of financial recklessness – as a rebellion against the prim and controlled person I had been. I gradually overextended myself financially and once again felt the pressure of being out of control. Fortunately my cheques never bounced once I had left my marriage, but my income was not enough to cover my expenses. For about a year now, however, I have been consolidating financially which feels so good! I can breathe easily and sleep well, and the end of the month or a trip to the supermarket is not a nightmare anymore.'

The therapist
A fair amount of time in therapy with depressed clients and people close to them is spent discussing and organising financial affairs. I enjoy financial planning and management in which I learn from, and teach, my clients. I also encourage a fair amount of discussion about how much money is enough. If an enormous amount is still not enough to satisfy a client, we look at deeper emotional thirsts because the desire for more money is likely to be the attempt to quench a thirst with salt water. It frequently transpires that this type of insatiable thirst is a function of feelings of nurture or love deprivation and/or a lack of spiritual or religious rootedness.

Summary
This section has highlighted the importance of financial management in coping with depression. We have also looked at the emotional meanings and associations that depressed clients and those close to them attach to money.

Summary

In Part 2 of this book I have suggested a variety of ways in which you can manage to live with depression. You may tell yourself that these methods apply to anyone, not only those who are depressed, or those close to someone who is depressed. That is a correct perception. It follows therefore that you include your choice of these coping mechanisms into your lifestyle from now on. My primary focus, however, has been to define successful self-help skills and to adapt them for use in a depressed system.

The message throughout this part of the book has been about taking good care of yourself, emotionally and physically, and by expressing your feelings through creativity as well as verbally.

I have suggested ways to reduce stress and lift depression actively such as physical exercise, and passively through deep muscle relaxation and the stimulation of the senses, including touch. I have emphasised the promotion of physical and emotional intimacy and the nutrition of both body and soul. Finally, I have discussed empowerment and control through financial management.

I have encouraged you to respect the depressed person for his or her decisions. In this way he or she moves from being 'sick', dependent and inferior to being a person with a mind of his or her own and an expert about his or her own needs and wants.

The person close to a depressed person will then be released from the awesome responsibility of 'care-taking' and curing the depressed person. You will have realised by now that attempts to take responsibility for the cure of depression are futile, and that all of the energy would be better utilised in rebuilding your own strength, while respecting the depressed person's ability to take responsibility for his or her own life decisions. This means that one stops 'care-taking', but does not stop caring about someone who is depressed. The position that I find most helpful in relation to a depressed person is to be one pace behind them. This is each one's own unique journey in which each has expert knowledge on how far, how fast and in which direction they wish to move and grow.

Also, remember the importance of time and timing in the process of change. Sometimes the timing is perfect and there is enormous and speedy change in both the depressed person and those close to him or her. At other times, one member of the depressed system is ready for change whilst the other is not. I have also, at times, seen a depressed client improve and thus become more confident – and less dependent – on those close to him or her. This can be quite frightening for close associates who have a strong need to be needed by the depressed 'patient'. The former no longer have a role to fulfil, and so might try to manoeuvre the previously depressed person back into the needy, inferior and sick position.

It is also important for you to recognise that you have *choices* in staying or leaving a depressed system. It might happen that someone close to a depressed person behaves destructively in an attempt to keep him or her 'ill' by not allowing attempts at health. It might become an option to leave (as seen in the case of Gina and Nick) if the depressed person refuses to acknowledge or take responsibility for the depression and living in that system has become destructive to close associates.

PART 3

MEDICAL APPROACH TO AND TREATMENT OF DEPRESSION

In Part 1 of this book I described depression. In Part 2 I offered you a repertoire of ideas and coping mechanisms for the self-management of depression. Please be aware that, while my focus has been on the management of depression, I have also offered fundamental ways of balancing your lifestyle forever, whether or not depression is present in your life. When depression exists and/or persists, the depression managers that I have offered should be incorporated into and continued along with any other treatment modality suggested in this book, or any others that you have found to work.

What follows in Part 3 are suggestions about medical treatments that are available for depression (psychotropic medication and electroshock therapy). You are, of course, at liberty to try or reject any of these on the basis that they 'fit' or do not 'fit' with the person that you are.

As a student conducting research on depression, and in my early years as a practising psychologist dealing with depressed people and those close to them, I had great difficulty in reconciling the medical treatments available for problems in daily life. Experience has tempered my views. This has happened over time as I have watched my clients struggling with debilitating manifestations of depression. There are antidepressants and/or tranquillising medications that clearly alleviate some of their symptoms and enrich the quality of their lives. The judicious use of medication also empowered and energised some of my clients so that they could benefit from psychotherapy and could begin to include some of the self-help methods described earlier in this book. I have also observed the beneficial effects of electroshock therapy in cases where self-help psychotherapy and medication are not effective and where the client remains 'stuck' in a terrible, deep, dark pit.

A great deal depends on the attitudes and belief-systems that the administrating doctors and other professionals hold about the depressed person and those close to them. The most benefit is derived when these value systems include:

- respect for the depressed client as an equal in the therapeutic relationship
- cognisance of the role of those close to the depressed person
- hearing the needs of the depressed client and close associates
- recognising when behaviour patterns of the depressed system are triggering the doctor's own unresolved issues
- flexibility in networking with other professionals to include the beneficial effects of other management methods together with the medical treatments
- observation of those factors and patterns operating in a depressed system that could have a psychological value in keeping the system depressed (more will be said about this in Part 4)
- discussion of effects and distressing or harmful side-effects of psychotropic medications

I work closely with several general practitioners and psychiatrists who treat their depressed clients and those close to them with respect and caring. These doctors share their areas of expertise with me to the benefit of our mutual clients. Although our areas of expertise are different, we are like-minded in terms of our attitudes towards our clients. I work with sensitive, perceptive professionals who feel comfortable about including themselves in a relationship with our clients and myself.

An example of what I mean about working constructively and including the medical treatment of depression with self-help, psychotherapy and homoeopathy was best expressed in a therapy session with me by Carly. She said, 'I was terribly anxious when you referred me to a psychiatrist. I thought that he and my family would regard me as a failure and mad. But as you had promised, he spoke to me as if he saw me as a person. He asked me for my input and my views on myself. He wanted to know what I needed.

He suggested to me that I be admitted to a private clinic for a rest. He readily heard me when I explained that lying in a hospital bed would make me feel more worthless than I already did. He suggested medication which he explained in terms of effects and side-effects, and answered the questions I asked about antidepressant options clearly. It seemed like a fortunate coincidence when an old friend, a medical doctor who practices homoeopathy, arrived from New Zealand for a visit and contacted me. She offered me a homoeopathic remedy that she assured me would not interfere with the antidepressants that my psychiatrist had prescribed. At first I felt wary about discussing this holistic treatment with the psychiatrist, but I've decided that he is so open and understanding about what I want that I am going to tell him about it. I will put him in contact with my homoeopath, so that they can answer each other's questions. What a relief!'

The reservations that I hold with respect to the medical model involve those medical professionals and psychiatric institutions where some of the following attitudes and belief-systems are still strongly evident:

- ignorance and/or condescension in attitude towards the role and needs of those people who are close to a depressed person
- use of an authoritarian, punitive, disrespectful and superior position in relation to the depressed person or those close to him or her
- rigid diagnosis of the depressed person into a category of depression that labels him or her and thereby perpetuates the 'illness'
- refusal to network with other professionals and to consider potentially beneficial alternative methods of management
- treatment of close associates as an intrusion in the therapy system
- maintenance of the depressed person in a dependent, non-coping role

Rob was referred to a psychiatrist by his general practitioner because a range of antidepressant medications had proved to be ineffective over a period of months. Sara described their experience to me: 'I had been invited to go with Rob to the psychiatrist's rooms. I was then instructed to stay in the waiting room for a while. I sat there for one and a half hours while he talked to Rob. I am furious that he did not even speak to me afterwards. I could just as well have dropped Rob off, gone to gym, and fetched him later.' Rob said, 'The psychiatrist didn't talk *to* me, he talked *at* me. Actually, he gave me a complicated lecture on how chemically sick I was and the complexities of making me well. I was shocked when he said that he wanted to admit me to a private psychiatric clinic where he thought I should be on a liquid diet (I made the mistake of telling him that I don't eat well. But then, I have never had a good appetite.) I refused to enter the clinic or to consult him again. I did take another week off work, but I stayed at home. I exercised, I visited my father's grave, talked to Sara and generally began to feel stronger. While I didn't like his attitude, I do believe that the new antidepressant that he had given me helped to lift my depression.'

Sometimes it is neccessary for a client to be hospitalised for depression. This is usually done when the client has become exhausted and too depressed to eat or, in fact, do anything.

I have included the medical treatments used for depression because, administered by knowledgeable, repectful and caring practitioners, they extend your choice of tools available in the management of depression. The first of these is the use of psychotropic medication.

PSYCHOTROPIC MEDICATION

I have decided to address this treatment choice by answering some of the questions most frequently asked by depressed clients and those close to them. I wish to stress that what follows is *not* a comprehensive guide to the actions – and interactions – of psychotropic medication in the treatment of depression. The aim is, rather, to describe the main groups of medication currently available for depression, with one or more examples of specific, commonly-used drugs belonging to each group. I have tried to explain these as clearly and simply as possible.

Q.
What are the main classes or categories of antidepressants – and other psychotropic drugs – presently available for the treatment of depression?

A.
- *tricyclic antidepressants*
  - amitriptyline (Elavil®; Trepiline®; Tryptanol®)
  - clomipramine (Anafranil®)
  - desipramine (Norpramin®; Pertofran®)
  - dothiepin, also called dosulepin (Prothiadin®; Thaden®)
  - imipramine (Ethipramine®; Tofranil®)
  - lofepramine (Emdalen®)
  - nortriptyline (Aventyl®)
  - trimipramine (Surmontil®; Tydamine®)

- *tetracyclic compounds*
  - maprotiline (Ludiomil®)
  - mianserin (Lantanon®)

- *selective serotonin re-uptake inhibitors (SSRIs)*
  - citalopram (Cipramil®)
  - fluoxetine (Prozac®)
  - fluvoxamine (Luvox®)
  - paroxetine (Aropax®; Paxil®)
  - sertraline (Zoloft®)
  - venlafaxine (Effexor®)

- *monoamine-oxidase inhibitors (MAOIs) – non-selective (irreversible)*
  - tranylcypromine (Parnate®)

- *monoamine-oxidase inhibitors (MAOIs) – selective Type A (reversible)*
  - moclobemide (Aurorix®)

- *benzodiazepine (non-sedative anxiolytic)*
  - alprazolam (Xanor®)

- *neuroleptics (also classified as psycholeptics or antipsychotics)*
  - flupent(h)ixol (Fluanxol®)
  - lithium carbonate (Camcolit®, Lentolith®)
  - sulpiride (Eglonyl®)

- *an antidepressant in a class of its own*
  - trazodone (Molipaxin®)

Q.
How do some of these psychotropic drugs work in the treatment of depression?
A.
Certain chemicals (termed *catecholamines*) exist between the synapses of the nerves (nerve endings). The catecholamines function as *neurotransmitters* and pass (transmit) messages throughout the nervous system. These catchelomines include *adrenaline* (also known as epinephrine), *noradrenaline* (norepinephrine) and *dopamine.*

As discussed in the section dealing with the diagnosis of depression, the research suggests that a partial or total depletion (re-uptake or absorption) of these catecholamines might cause depression.

Another important neurotransmitter involved in depression is 5-hydroxytryptamine (5-HT), better known as *SEROTONIN*). As with the catecholamines, the research indicates that the re-uptake or a deficiency of *serotonin* could cause depression.[1]

Further research suggests that *increased* amounts of steroids (17-hydrocorticoid), sodium and potassium between the nerve endings are present with depression.[2]

- *tricyclic antidepressants*
  These antidepressants seem to work by inhibiting the re-uptake (depletion) of the neurotransmitters – serotonin, adrenaline and noradrenaline at the synapses between the nerve cells.[3] These, in general, have antidepressant and sedative (calming) effects on the client.

- *tetracyclic compounds*
  These antidepressants work in much the same way as the tricyclics in that they operate to inhibit or prevent the re-uptake of neurotransmitters. They work mainly on adrenaline and noradrenaline, and not on serotonin.

- *5-HT (selective serotonin re-uptake inhibitors – SSRIs):*
  As their name indicates, these antidepressants work specifically and selectively to inhibit the re-uptake (absorption or depletion) of *serotonin* between the nerve endings.[4] These antidepressants do not seem to work well when the client is both depressed and

highly anxious. They do not have a sedative effect. Therefore, when anxiety is high, it is probably better to use one of the tricyclics.

- *monoamine oxidase inhibitors (MAOIs)*
  It is believed that the enzyme 'monoamine oxidase' inactivates the neurotransmitters, adrenaline, noradrenaline and serotonin. The reason for the use of the MAOIs is that they prevent or inhibit the action of the monoamine oxidase enzyme and, in so doing, serotonin, adrenaline and noradrenaline levels increase. The MAOIs (non-selective) such as tranylcypromine (Parnate®) have many side-effects that are potentially dangerous, and are contra-indicated when combined with certain medications and foods containing tyramine. (For examples of some of these medications and foods see side-effects of monoamine oxidase inhibitors – non-selective on page 99.) For these reasons, the non-selective MAOIs are only used when other antidepressants do not work, and then only very carefully, with explanation to the client of their effects and side-effects. The advantage of the selective (Type A) MAOIs such as moclobemide (Aurorix®) is the reduced dangers when combined with certain foods. Aurorix® reversibly inhibits monoamine oxidase Type A resulting in increased concentrations of serotonin, adrenaline and noradrenaline.

- *benzodiazepines*
  These are, in fact, tranquillisers (anxiolytics). One of these has been included, viz. alprazolam (Xanor®) because it seems to work to reduce anxiety and at the same time to have antidepressant properties. Alprazolam (Xanor®) is not a sedative tranquilliser, but rather acts by facilitating the action of gamma-aminobutyric acid (GABA), a major inhibitory neurotransmitter in the central nervous system. Sometimes these drugs are combined with one of the non-sedative antidepressants. Generally benzodiazepines can cause dependence.

- *neuroleptics (antipsychotics or psycholeptics)*
  These psychotropic drugs are designed for the treatment of psychoses. Some of them, taken in low doses, work effectively to reduce depression and to decrease levels of anxiety. Generally, serotonin mechanisms at a variety of serotonin receptor sites are

the targets for neuroleptics. *Flupent(h)ixol* (Fluanxol®) is one example. These neuroleptics are sometimes used in combination with an antidepressant.
– A drug commonly used in the treatment of severe manic-depression (bipolar affective disorders) is *lithium carbonate* (Camcolit®, Lentolith®). This is an inorganic chemical compound. It has a sedative effect on the client suffering from manic-depression. Levels of lithium in the blood must be regularly monitored because when these levels are too high, death could occur through toxicity.
– *sulpiride* (Eglonyl®) works to stimulate or produce more dopamine (a catecholamine neurotransmitter)

- *antidepressants that are in a class of their own*
  – trazodone (Molipaxin®) does not appear to influence the re-uptake of noradrenaline and dopamine.

For further information on the actions of the various psychotropic drugs used in depression, see the list of references at the back of this book. You could also speak to your general practitioner, pharmacist, psychiatrist or psychologist for answers to your questions. Do not hesitate to ask. You are the person taking the drugs!

Q. *What are some of the more commonly-experienced side-effects of anti-depressants?*
A.
- *tricyclics*
  – low blood pressure
  – weight gain
  – mental fogginess
  – constipation
  – hands shaking
  – lowered sexual desire
  – dizziness
  – blurred vision
  – dry mouth
  – sleeplessness
  – drowsiness
  – urine retention, or difficulty starting to urinate
  – skin reactions

- *tetracyclics*
  - drowsiness

- *5-HT (serotonin re-uptake inhibitors – SSRIs)*
  - insomnia if taken later than early morning
  - nausea and vomiting
  - decreased appetite
  - agitation
  - lowered sexual desire and difficulty achieving orgasm

- *monoamine oxidase inhibitors (MAOIs) – non-selective (irreversible)*
  - low blood pressure
  - confusion
  - ankle swelling
  - dry mouth
  - weakness
  - urinary difficulties
  - skin rash
  - agitation
  - dizziness
  - weight gain
  - insomnia
  - drowsiness
  - dietary restrictions due to severe high blood pressure when combined with alcohol and foods containing tyramine. Restricted foods include bananas, broad beans, Marmite, Bovril, Oxo, caviar, cheese, chicken liver, yeast extracts, chocolate, pickled herring. This is not a comprehensive list.
  - restricted use of certain other drugs – such as amphetamines, certain analgesics, cough mixtures, appetite suppressants, barbiturates, sedatives and antidiabetics. Please check what these are.
  - craving for carbohydrates that could result in weight gain
  - lowered sexual desire and difficulty achieving orgasm

- *monoamine oxidase inhibitors (MAOIs) – selective (reversible) Type A*
  - sleep disturbances
  - dizziness
  - nausea
  - vomiting

- headaches
- confusion
- agitation
- constipation
- anxiety
- restlessness
- dry mouth
- diarrhoea
- loss of appetite
- hypotension may occur

While dietary restrictions are not as important with these reversible MAOIs, clients should avoid consuming large quantities of alcohol and food containing tyramine and restrict the use of certain medications. Please discuss any necessary dietary and medication restrictions with your doctor.

- *neuroleptics (antipsychotics)*
  - weakness
  - drowsiness
  - depression
  - skin irritations
  - anxiety
  - tardive dyskinesia and tardive dystonia with prolonged use. Tardive dyskinesia results in uncontrollable movement (from twitches to severe jerking movements). Tardive dystonia involves severe and painful muscle spasm with distortion and twisting of body parts.

Please discuss the side-effects that you may experience with your doctor. The above list is not comprehensive.

Q.
What can you do to cope better with some of the more frequently experienced side-effects of antidepressants and neuroleptics (antipsychotics)?
A.
- *weight gain*
  - See section on nutrition.
  - Keep to a diet high in complex carbohydrates (grains and vegetables)

- Avoid food high in sugars and fats.
- Your doctor may change your medication to one of the SSRIs.

- *constipation*
  - Drink eight glasses of water a day.
  - Eat high-fibre foods and salads every day.
  - Exercise regularly.
  - Ask your doctor for a bulk-producing fibre agent.
  - Avoid laxatives.

- *water retention*
  - Decrease intake of salt.

- *nausea*
  - Take medication with milk or food.

- *urinating difficulties*
  - If it takes longer than five minutes to start a stream of urine, tell your doctor.

- *shaking hands or tremors*
  - Drink sufficient amounts of fluids.
  - Use relaxation exercises.
  - Soak in a warm bath or in a jacuzzi (if available).

- *dry mouth*
  - Visit your dentist more often than usual for tooth and gum hygiene.
  - Drink water or other fluids on a frequent basis.
  - Ask your doctor or dentist about medication that acts to stimulate saliva, as well as the possible side-effects of this drug.
  - Chew sugarless gum or sugarless sucking sweets.
  - Use a fluoride rinse to prevent tooth decay.
  - Brush teeth regularly.

- *tardive dyskinesia and tardive dystonia*
  - These side-effects may occur after long-term use of certain neuroleptics (anti-psychotic drugs).
  - There is no cure.
  - Symptoms may be reduced by stress management including

relaxation exercises, hot baths, application of ice or moist heat for pain and acute symptoms.
– Exercise to improve muscle tone and posture.

- *dizziness*
  – Move slowly when climbing stairs, getting out of bed or standing up from a chair.
  – Eat sufficient salt on a daily basis.
  – Drink a lot of water.
  – Avoid extreme changes in temperature.
  – Tell your doctor if the dizziness is severe.

- *drowsiness*
  – You will most probably find that drowsiness passes when you have been on the antidepressant for a while.
  – Be careful not to drive or use dangerous machinery whilst drowsy.

- *lowered sexual desire, impotence and difficulty achieving orgasm*
  – No treatment exists for lowered sexual desire except for lowered dosage, or a change to a different type of antidepressant. Some clients stop medication for this reason. Discuss this problem with your doctor.
  – Certain medications are useful with difficulty in achieving orgasms. These include Periactin®, Urecholine® and Symmetrel®. Ask your doctor about these.

- *insomnia*
  – Try to get into the habit of going to bed at the same time every night.
  – Take sedative antidepressant medication one or two hours before you go to bed.
  – Take antidepressant medication that keeps you awake in the morning.
  – You might find that a herbal tea such as camomile helps.

The depressed client
My clients fall into two general categories:

- those who are already, or have previously been on psychotropic medication
- those who are on no medication

In both of these cases, clients talk a great deal about medication. The majority do not like the idea of taking 'drugs' and the fact that they may become dependent on these drugs. I explain that antidepressants are not generally addictive, but benzodiazepines are. My clients often feel that they may be seen as weak-willed because they need a psychological crutch. If they are on medication, they generally want to know how quickly they will be able to stop taking the 'dreaded' chemicals.

This depends on the type of drug. We also discuss the presence or absence of side-effects which are usually short-lived. If there are severe and/or prolonged side-effects it may be indicative that another drug is necessary or that psychotropic medication needs to be stopped. I listen to my client's point of view and answer as many questions as I am able. When I do not know the answers, I contact the prescribing doctor, or suggest that my client does, for answers to questions. I am in contact with our Medicines' Information Centre where there are experts on drug actions and interactions for professionals who require advice.

Close associates
Sometimes those close to a depressed person are anxious or insistent that the latter take antidepressants. This is either to make living with a depressed person easier, or because they really believe this medication to be the answer.

There are also close associates who are vehemently against the idea that the depressed person needs 'pills'. The message to the depressed person is that they must throw away the 'poison', and sort themselves out.

Another group of clients who are close to a depressed person feel so depressed and anxious in the depressed system that they ask for psychotropic medication in order to cope with the situation. Sara became tearful and developed sleep and eating disturbances. Rob's general practitioner then prescribed Prozac® and Xanor® for Sara. She reported feeling much calmer and more energised once she began taking the medication.

The therapist
I have observed my clients, both depressed people and those close to them, while they have been taking psychotropic medication. I have not generally seen dramatic changes, but rather subtle effects, or no change at all. The clients who benefit seem to think more clearly, to sleep better, to eat better and to be less weepy. When there is no change, or when the side-effects are prolonged and intolerable, I generally suggest that they discuss these problems with the prescribing doctor with a view to reducing the dose, changing or stopping medication. When they change to another medication, I explain that they may need to wait for one to five weeks to see results, depending on the time the new medication takes to work. Some of these drugs take time to work out of the system. This time is termed the 'half-life' of the drug. The 'half-life' of the drug must be considered when medication is changed or stopped.

Summary
In this section I have explored the general classes of medication available in the treatment of depression. It is important that you know that you have the right to ask as many questions as you choose about the effects, side-effects and interactions of these drugs with anything else that you may be taking. Besides your doctor and psychologist, your pharmacist should be able to answer many of your questions and provide you with information about the medication that you are taking. You are absolutely at liberty to stop medication that you do not feel is helping you, or that you experience as harmful. Please discuss this with your doctor as it may be necessary to cut down slowly, rather than stop the medication abruptly. You should never feel pressured to take medication if you are against the idea. In this case, however, you should listen to the potential benefits and side-effects before making a decision.

ELECTROSHOCK THERAPY (ECT)

If, in my early years as a student and as a practitioner, I was against the idea of psychotropic medication for depression, I was even more against the idea of ECT. I worried about the client's memory loss and confusion. I also frequently heard close associates reminding the depressed person about their 'shock' treatment, and how they were mentally defective because of the need for this treatment and because of the effects that it would have on them.

As I have continued to work in the field of depression, I have seen that ECT sometimes works to improve the depressed person's quality of life, and to relieve severe depression. When ECT works, it does so quickly (within two to three weeks). Memory loss, however, is often reported after treatment. When it does not work, the depressed person feels no better. I have heard clients say that their first course of treatment felt like a magic cure whilst a subsequent course of treatment was useless.

My present attitude is that if anything works to make a depressed person feel better (including ECT), then it should be used when indicated.

QUESTIONS ASKED ABOUT ECT

Q.
When is ECT indicated?
A.
- when psychotropic medication is not working, and the client is unable to eat
- when the client is under pressure to improve quickly, as in the case of pregnancy or certain impending social, family or occupational events
- with severe depression and/or mania
- when the depressed client is unable to tolerate the side-effects of antidepressants

Q.
When is ECT contra-indicated?
A.
- with brain tumours. Here, ECT appears to bring about rapid physical and mental deterioration. Speak to your doctor about other contra-indications of ECT.

Q.
What happens to the client who has ECT?

A.
- The client receives a full explanation of 'procedure' as well as potential benefits, dangers and side-effects.
- There will be a request for the client's consent, which may be withdrawn at any time.
- An opportunity will be given to receive answers to any questions.
- A full physical examination with electro-cardiogram, chest x-ray, urine and blood tests will be done.
- A course of ECT generally involves six to twelve treatments on alternate days, with no food or drink consumed for eight hours before each treatment.
- Medications are given intravenously that will reduce saliva, induce sleep and relax the muscles.
- When medications have taken effect, electric current is passed through the brain by means of electrodes.
- These electrical stimuli seem to produce EEG (brain wave) changes that are similar to a *grand mal* seizure (convulsion). These convulsions, over a series of treatments, seem to bring about improvement in depression.
- The client will wake up about 30 minutes after treatment.
- The client will feel confused on waking up but soon re-orientates him or herself.

Q.
How long do the benefits of ECT last?
A.
- Benefits generally last for about six months.
- Some other form of treatment for depression should follow ECT to prevent relapses.

Q.
Does ECT result in brain damage?
A.
- No evidence of brain damage exists.
- Memory loss for a few months or longer has been reported.

The depressed client
Two of my clients received *ECT* on two separate occasions some years before consulting with me. They both reported marked

improvement after the first course of treatment, but no improvement after the second series of treatment. Both reported 'blanks' in their memory. Both patients had relapsed after the first treatments. Also, neither had continued with any form of treatment for depression after the ECT, and this could explain the relapses.

Close associates
In both of the above cases, my clients were married women in their 30s. The first client's husband used the fact that his wife had had ECT to criticise her and confirm for himself that she was 'mad'. In the second case, the client's husband was caring and concerned, and fully accepted any treatment (including ECT) that might make his wife feel better.

The therapist
For me, ECT exists as a mode of treatment for severe depression and/or mania as a last resort. My dilemma, however, is that prevention of a relapse is often dependent on concurrent use of an antidepressant. Should the client suffer severe side-effects from antidepressants, the initial beneficial effects of ECT might be short-lived.

Summary
In this section I have examined the potential benefits, dangers and side-effects of ECT.

As with psychotropic medication, you must ask questions about everything that you want to know. You may also refuse treatment by this means, or terminate treatment at any time.

SUMMARY

I have discussed the medical approach to depression in an attempt to highlight its obvious benefits and disadvantages. It is clear that this approach is useful when used within a constructive and respectful therapeutic relationship between the client, those close to him or her, the doctor, the psychologist and the staff of the in-patient clinic or hospital (when indicated). As discussed at the beginning of Part 3, the converse of the above could render this approach less than helpful, or even harmful to the depressed client and close associates.

PART 4

PSYCHOTHERAPY WITH DEPRESSION

By this time you are *au fait* with how my clients, those close to them and I describe depression. You will have used methods from this book and/or your own means to describe your unique experience of depression (Part 1). I hope that you have investigated, or intend practising, some of the self-help methods examined in Part 2. You may also have agreed and/or disagreed with some of my views on the medical treatment of depression. Perhaps you have had some of your questions answered on medication and/or ECT. Possibly, this has generated further questions that you wish to ask your doctor and/or psychotherapist.

At best, you are already feeling better. At worst, you have food for thought and for use at some time in the future.

My intention in this part of the book is to give you an overview of some of the theories and methods of psychotherapy that are commonly used with depression (psychoanalytic, behavioural, cognitive, interpersonal and systems).

WHAT ARE SOME OF THE PSYCHOLOGICAL THEORIES AND THERAPIES USED IN THE TREATMENT OF DEPRESSION?

PSYCHOANALYTIC APPROACH TO DEPRESSION

This approach sees depression as being caused in early childhood, by the loss of an object of love (such as mother, through death, rejection or disappointment)[1]. This loss results in a particular vulnerability in childhood. Later in life, this person will regress to a childhood state of vulnerability and depression whenever faced with life crises and tensions.[2] It is also believed that depression results from repressed anger/hostility or guilt, and a reversion to the loss experienced by the person at the oral stage of development (from birth to two years)[3].

In the course of this therapy, the depressed client lies on a couch and says whatever comes to mind. This is called 'free association'. The therapist interprets these spoken associations in terms of unpleasant childhood experiences (losses) which are in the client's unconscious mind and are causing the depression. Any positive (or negative) feelings that the client expresses towards the therapist are explained as part of the establishment of a *transference relationship*.[4] The *transference relationship* between therapist and client is explained as feelings that the client has had towards important people in his or her life. These feelings are transferred onto the therapist. The establishment of this *transference relationship* is fundamental to the success of therapy[5]. The feelings most frequently expressed in this relationship are those of hostility, dependence, manipulation for care and attention and insensitivity to the feelings of others. If the client is unable to express these feelings during the therapy he or she is said to be 'resitant'. This resistance must be worked through in therapy so that a *transference relationship* can be established. The client will then gain insight into the cause of his or her depression and be cured. The therapist takes on a passive role and is not viewed as a 'real person' with his or her own feelings during therapy. If the therapist does feel and express his or her own feelings in therapy, this is regarded as *counter transference* that must be eliminated. The therapist must then work through these feelings in his or her own therapy.

BEHAVIOURAL APPROACH TO DEPRESSION

This approach sees depression as having been learned and reinforced through conditioning. Here, the depressed person is thought to have been rewarded by important people throughout his or her life, for depressive-type behaviours[6]. The reason for this is that the individual does not seem to show sufficient positive behaviours that others could reinforce.[7] Another belief within this approach is that a person becomes depressed because there is not enough reinforcement (either negative or positive) of his or her behaviours. Sometimes there are no reinforcements at all of behaviours because a significant reinforcing person (such as a mother) has died. A third theory is that reinforcements of (positive or negative) behaviours occur in an inconsistent manner (randomly). The person realises that he or she is helpless in his or her bid to obtain approval and satisfaction from important people. It is thought that depression is learned maladaptive behaviour where the depressive behaviour limits the behavioural repertoire of the person[8].

One effective approach to the treatment of depression is assertiveness training. This technique involves the direct and honest communication of thoughts and feelings. It is aimed at socially acceptable communication, which does not hurt the feelings of others[9]. Another means of treatment is to advise family members to reinforce only coping, non-depressed behaviours and to ignore depressed, non-coping behaviours. The hope is that the depressed behaviours will disappear and the non-depressed behaviours will increase[10]. Another treatment for the anxiety associated with depression is the deep muscle relaxation discussed earlier in this book.

COGNITIVE APPROACH TO DEPRESSION

The essence of this approach is that a person becomes depressed because his or her thinking is faulty (irrational). These thoughts are negative and bring about depressive moods. Aaron Beck developed this theory and therapy which explains depression in terms of the 'cognitive triad'. Here people think of themselves, their worlds and the future in a distorted or negative manner[11]. Cognitive therapy aims to correct these negative thought patterns. This correction of faulty thinking is believed to cure depression[12]. This approach has contributed greatly to the understanding and treatment of depression. It is worth reading the relevant literature on cognitive therapy.

INTERPERSONAL APPROACH TO DEPRESSION

This approach views maladaptive behaviour, including depression, as faulty verbal (and especially non-verbal) behaviours in relationships. These behaviours include:

- 'head-in-hands' posture
- feelings and expressions of helplessness, hopelessness, despair and depression
- slowness of speech and movement
- monotonous tone of voice
- unpleasant facial expression
- 'down in the mouth' behaviour
- avoidance of eye-contact

There is not as much concern with *what* the client expresses, but rather *how* these behaviours, thoughts and feelings are expressed, and how these expressions impact on family members, friends and work associates[13]. This approach suggests that all behaviours, including depressive behaviours, do not exist in isolation, but have a function or psychological value in the social system of the depressed person. It does not, however, deny the pain experienced by the depressed person. The depressed person's behaviour is seen as rigid, where the position of each person in a relationship is carefully maintained. Depression usually starts with normal feelings and expressions of sadness or loss. If these expressions continue for too long, the result is that people around the depressed person begin to see him or her as psychologically inferior and unable to cope. With time, the depressed person comes to believe that he or she is inferior in all relationships, even those that have nothing to do with the cause of the depression. This rigid, depressed behaviour continues even though it causes the person great pain. The reason for continuing this behaviour is that it elicits predictable, familiar and therefore safe responses from others. These responses include: sympathy, caretaking or caring feelings and/or irritation and frustration. This type of depressed behaviour will, therefore, limit the way in which others respond to the depressed person.

In therapy, the depressed client usually communicates by using his or her depressive symptoms, as this is the way that he or she has tried to gain acceptance and approval from others. The depressed behaviour, however, does not elicit the approval and acceptance that the depressed client needs. It does bring forth conflicting feelings and behaviours from others (sympathy and irritation, caring and rejection, responsibility and resentment).

The therapist must therefore discover *how* the client interacts by using his or her depressive symptoms, and not *why* he or she interacts this way. The therapist observes the way in which the client interacts in the therapy and how he or she complains about important people in his or her system. To achieve this, the therapist offers warmth, empathy and honesty. These are elements developed by Carl Rogers in client-centered therapy. In this safe therapeutic climate, the client feels free to express and explore his or her feelings in a non-threatened way. The therapist then becomes more active and assertive in communicating with the client in an attempt to define and clarify the problem/s. The therapist will also try to discover the psychological value that the symptoms have in the depressed person's social systems. The therapist will show the client how his or her style of behaviour is related to his or her difficulties in relationships. The therapeutic relationship offers the client flexible, alternative ways of communicating. In therapy, therefore, the depressed person's symptoms are no longer serving a purpose or having a value. Thus the depressed person will start to behave differently. Therapy is aimed at promoting honest and direct communication, first in the safe context of the therapy relationship, and later outside of therapy.

A Systems approach to depression

The therapies mentioned thus far (psychoanalytic, behavioural, cognitive and interpersonal) each offer various techniques for the treatment of depression. The systems approach serves as a broad structure or framework within which one or more, or other means described earlier in the book, may effectively be used with depression.

The purpose of using various therapeutic methods within this framework is to attempt to drastically alter the complex web of interactions that maintain and continue depressive symptoms in the depressed client's system. Therefore, when described from a systems point of view, the treatment of depression is limited only by the boundaries on creativity of the therapist! It has been suggested that depression develops from unresolved grief[14]. Others[15] described patterns of behaviour exisiting in the marital system while further research describes the operation of a family system that is depressed[16].

The therapist will observe some of the following patterns in depressed systems:

- Painful feelings are expressed that relate to grief, disappointment and loss.
- The client speaks slowly and monotonously, with a low voice pitch.
- The client shows little body movement.
- There are frequent, tension-producing silences.
- The client talks a lot about him or herself.
- The client frequently asks for reassurance and sympathy.
- Close associates respond with reassurance and sympathy (by a 'soft-talking' caretaker), or more aggressively (by a 'tough-talking' caretaker).
- Behaviours exist to confirm guilt, dissatisfaction and complaints.
- Depressed systems prevent personal growth of the members.
- Members of depressed systems are usually isolated from other outside systems.
- Guilt is provoked.
- Responsibility is avoided.
- Power struggles for control exist in these systems.
- The role of the depressed client in these systems is often alternated. When the depressed person gets better, someone else in the system gets depressed.
- One member is usually defined as the coping, concerned, caretaker, whilst another member of the system is the 'ill', weak, dependent, non-coper.
- The concern of one of the members maintains the depressed person in a psychologically inferior position.
- Any attempt for independence by a member of these systems is sabotaged by the other member/s.
- Other behaviours in the depressed systems include: passive aggression, hostility, isolation, harassing of the members, sacrifice, and scape-goating.
- Depressive behaviours in a system mutually complement each other in such a way that they fit together. The complementary behaviours often involve opposites – inferior versus superior roles of marital partners, depressed and non-depressed spouses.

The therapist takes note of how the behaviours in a depressed system are maintaining and continuing the symptoms and the value or purpose of these symptoms in keeping the system depressed[17].

The therapist could use psychoanalytic interpretation to work through grief and thus facilitate the movement of the system towards constructive growth[18]. Ideally, intensive individual therapy as well as marital therapy are used when depression exists in a marital system[19]. The individual therapy should focus on the individual's depressed style of interacting in systems, while the marital therapy should examine and change the rigid roles of the members of this system.

The therapist must be fully aware of his or her own behaviour in the system to avoid getting 'sucked in' to the system and thus preserving and perpetuating the depression.

In simplistic terms, then, after defining the symptoms maintaining and perpetuating patterns in the depressed system, the therapist may use any technique/s available, or create his or her own means to 'shake' the depressed system, so that it will find new ways of functioning.

In general, I use the systems approach in psychotherapy with depression. It gives me the opportunity to use whatever works, from a broad repertoire of treatments that are available. Also, this approach includes the therapist as an active member of the therapy system. This fits with my 'hands on' style in therapy as well as my need to use whatever works. My methods include:

- the self-help techniques described earlier
- networking with members of the medical profession when necessary
- the techniques of psychotherapy explained in this part of the book
- an exploration of some of the holistic methods of therapy available for depression (Part 5)

For the rest of this part of the book, you are invited to join me on an interesting and challenging journey through therapy with a depressed client, Carly, and those close to her. This case study will illustrate how I work in a systems way with depression.

Carly

Carly is 35 years old. She is married and has an eight-year-old daughter. She is a personnel consultant in partnership with a single woman of about the same age.

Carly had attended one of my stress management workshops. She subsequently consulted with me for psychotherapy for severe stress and alcohol abuse. She described an eight-year history during which she had suffered two long and debilitating depressive episodes. One of these had followed her emigration to Australia, away from her large close-knit family of origin. This first episode had occured after the birth of her daughter in Australia, and the second experience of depression had been associated with grief after her second child was born. This baby had been diagnosed with a terminal illness. He had lived for a year, after which he had died. In addition, Carly's father had had a motor car accident the same year and had become an invalid. Her mother had recently recovered from a long and severe depression. Her sister (also her best friend) had gone to live in America for a period of two years.

When she first came to consult me, no-one other than Carly's husband, her mother and her sister knew of her inability to control her drinking. She was particularly concerned for her future as both her brothers were alcoholics. Carly explained to me that she had worked through her last depression in therapy, but she was still taking Prozac® to fortify herself against a relapse. She explained that she had always been a person of excesses: too much alcohol, too much food with an associated weight gain, too much work, and so on.

She described her relationship with her husband, James, as good. (He was kind and caring, and he willingly took on many of the household chores.) She had not, however, shared her deepest feelings with him – especially about the loss of their baby. She had felt more comfortable sharing these emotions with her mother, sister and certain close women friends. This had upset James and he felt left out when she did not include him in her confidences. He had also complained that their sex life was arid. She had had no interest in sex.

Carly's perception of her life
'I grew up in a very close-knit, religious family. I am one of five siblings. We all knew that hard work and achievement was valued. My parents had always done everything together. In fact, I would say that, until my father was paralysed, he had done everything for my mother. He was also kind and helpful to everyone that he knew, including his children. I think that my mother's depression started when my father became an invalid. She then had to take responsibility for all the tasks previously taken care of by my dad. Another reason has obviously been the terrible loss of our baby, their grandchild. She has also been deeply upset by the wreck one of my brothers has made of his life through being a "down and out" alcoholic. In my family, when one of us was in pain, we all wept.

'I feel riddled with guilt. How could I have left the responsibility of the business to Sally (her business partner) when I was depressed after Jeremy's death? I will never be able to show enough gratitude to her for that time. I try to be kind and understanding with my staff, but with James I let out all my angers and irritations. He hardly ever retaliates. I feel guilty about this but can't seem to help myself. I am not a good mother to Melanie; I'm so tired all the time that I don't think I give her enough "quality" time. I often retreat to my bed to lie under my duvet at the end of a tough day at work. I spend most weekends in bed, I think to recover from the week. To be honest, I also stay in bed when I have drunk a lot the previous night. This is not how a good wife and mother ought to be. James and I never go out to a restaurant or movies. Finance is tight and this makes me feel insecure. Sally and I generate a lot of income from the business, but we have bought expensive fixed assets. We pay our staff well, and thus have decided to draw small monthly salaries for ourselves. Paradoxically, I have no problem spending huge amounts on alcohol every week. I sometimes buy wine at the bottle store, but more often than not the bottle store is closed. I will buy expensive wine from a restaurant. Some evenings, I do my paperwork into the early hours of the morning. I know that I'm only able to do this with the help of alcohol. I don't get rolling drunk, but the next day my head is thick and I crave Coca Colas and rich, fatty foods. This just adds to my rapidly spreading girth and doesn't help my ability to think clearly.

'In the past, I have known what to do to help myself, but this time I somehow keep sabotaging my efforts. I feel that it is now time for me to get my life in order. I want to stop drinking, lose weight, give more quality time to Melanie and work on my relationship with James. I want to work in a balanced and productive way in my business. I am frightened to commit myself to any of these goals because I think that I might fail. I know, however, that they are all essential. Perhaps, I should start by cutting out the alcohol. It's the one thing that makes me feel bad and out of control of my life.'

Questions I needed to ask Carly
In the early stage of therapy, I wanted to know how Carly described herself. What were her immediate problems? I also needed to understand her current relationships with her husband and child, her family of origin, her business partner and staff, clients and her friends. In addition, I asked for information on her childhood and adolescence. I needed to learn about the types of relationships that she had had with her parents, her siblings and the people who had made up her world. Further important information included her culture, religious beliefs and values and belief-systems held by her family of origin. It was valuable to ascertain how past patterns of thoughts, feelings and behaviour were being continued into the present, some constructively, others destructively. I was also looking at Carly's patterns of behaviour and those closest to her that might have the psychological value of keeping her 'stuck'.

What I did to elicit this information
I started by asking Carly what recent problems had brought her to me. Then I told her that I would ask her many questions about herself and her difficulties. I explained that we would discuss her history in order to understand her present difficulties better. To this end, I created a therapeutic climate characterised by the qualities of the therapist as proposed by Carl Rogers, in his 'client-centred' and 'person-centred' psychotherapy. This type of therapy falls within the framework of the 'interpersonal approach' to depression[20]. These therapeutic qualities are: warmth, empathy and congruence (honesty). This therapeutic climate is conducive to a trust-relationship developing between my client and myself. She

would gradually be able to feel safe enough to reveal herself (positive aspects as well as negative) at deeper and deeper levels. This would happen later in therapy.

What I saw and felt in the early stages of this therapy
Carly sat opposite me in my consulting rooms with her arms folded. She looked terribly angry. Her eyes were clouded. She was polite to me and did not express any verbal anger towards anyone about whom she was speaking. What she did express was great shame, guilt and embarrassment at the fact that she had taken time off work after her baby had died and burdened her partner with extra responsibility. She cowered and hung her head when she talked of this 'sin'. Her shame and self-loathing were even more evident when she spoke of her inability to control alcohol. Carly presented herself as a person trying to gain control over her environment. At the same time, she looked as if she were protecting and defending her very sensitive soul. She did not, at this stage, show me her pain. She was, however, showing high levels of stress.

What I offered besides warmth, empathy and congruence
I suggested various means of stress management in order for Carly to achieve a sense of coping with her life. These included exercise, relaxation (using my deep muscle relaxation cassette), and I advised her to say 'No!' to unreasonable requests. I asked her to consciously take space for herself (not under the duvet, unless that space was free of guilt and perceived as positive). I also suggested that she make a collage to clarify how she felt at that time and what she wanted for herself in the future.

How my suggestions worked for Carly
'I have been walking briskly for 20 minutes, three times a week for the past two weeks. My head has become clearer. I really feel less stressed. I have also been avoiding my duvet as a retreat. Instead I have been been doing some fun things with Melanie. I'm more relaxed with her and she seems to be responding well to me. I have been asking James to take care of Melanie while I 'take space' alone in nature, now and then. James and I are not talking much about anything important, just practical issues. We are still not having sex at all. He told me long ago that he won't initiate love-making

any more because he hates to be rejected. I don't want to make the first move. Before I get into that, I want to work on my drinking. I am going to stop. I have decided to join Alcoholics Anonymous. I'll go to my first meeting next week. Do you see this collage? One side is full of excesses – alcohol, rich food, partying. Now look at the other side: all those soothing things – trees, water, time with family. This side feels so soothing. I'm getting there and for the first time, I don't think I'm going to sabotage my own healthy growth.'

Some thoughts of mine
I watched Carly work things out for herself. I kept pace with her – not too fast and not too slow. I was very restrained on the topic of alcohol. I knew that time was her best ally in reaching the point at which she stopped drinking. She was using me as a mirror for her move towards the management of her stress and her life. I saw her gradually feel better about herself. Her eyes became brighter and her guilt lessened. She spoke to me more positively about herself and her future. I was, however, concerned about the growing distance between her husband and herself.

What was I doing?
I was slowly becoming more active in a therapeutic situation. I began to challenge Carly when she expressed irrational negativity about herself. I also involved Carly in assertiveness training where she learned to 'dump' her guilt. We discussed her relationships with her parents and siblings. I could feel her strong sense of belonging and safety with her parental family. I brought up the relationship between herself and James, but she resisted this issue.

What was Carly doing?
'I'm feeling strong physically and emotionally, from the regular walks which also give me space. I've been seeing you for four months now, and going to AA meetings regularly for about three. I haven't stopped drinking, but the group support is amazing and very non-judgemental. A man told me he didn't stop drinking for a whole year. I must stop in my own time. I don't feel bad any more. I still binge-drink but much less than before. The best thing is that my sister is arriving home next week. I can't wait. She will be pleased to see me so much more relaxed and happy. You know, I

can talk to her about absolutely anything. Oh, by the way, James and I have started making love. We talk to each other much more and it feels good. We are still a bit wary of each other. I think that our distance from each other began when we could not share our grief at the loss of our baby. On the work front, I feel good that I am doing my fair share again. I've got so much more energy.'

Six months later
Until now, Carly had talked dispassionately to me about her post-natal depression and the loss of her baby, as well as her depression in Australia. She spoke of these things as if they had been resolved. I accepted her stance. My style in therapy is to journey with my client and not to presume that they are feeling what I think they ought to be thinking or feeling. She was now looking good, with an excited twinkle in her eyes. Carly had lost weight. Her shoulders were well back and she was speaking to and connecting with me. She had been taking Prozac® from the time of her baby's death but now felt ready to stop.

How Carly felt
'I am weaning myself off Prozac®. I'm ready to stop drinking and I've chosen the Christmas period to do so. As an extra help, I'm going to take Antabuse®, for a year if necessary, to make sure that I don't start drinking again. This will give my body and mind a chance to get used to life without the crutch of alcohol.'

How her grief surfaced
Carly was now virtually free of alcohol, save for a few lapses. She chose to accept these lapses as normal and did not castigate herself after a binge. The occasional binges were, in fact, positive, in that they confirmed for her that she was no longer in the frame of mind to drink.

Finally, the long-buried pain and guilt came flooding to the surface. Carly needed to be free from alcohol before she could face her pain. It is interesting that many of my clients are truly able to face their demons when they are feeling strong. At this stage, Carly was well able to cope with her life. From this base, she could move to the deeper levels of her soul. In therapy, she cried for the first time as she talked about her baby's illness and death.

Carly faces her pain
'I remember the pain and helplessness of being told that my small baby was so ill that he would die. There was nothing that I could do to save him. Worse for me than my pain was watching him in pain. A mother should not have to lose a child and a child should not have to suffer. A good mother should be able to protect her young. I couldn't. I just drank and drank to obliterate the terrible reality of what was happening. As if that wasn't bad enough, I would drink heavily at night so that I could sleep. Often I did not hear my baby crying for comfort and reassurance. James had to go to him on these nights, and I would wake up groggy and with a headache the next day. How could I have done this to my own baby?

'To make matters even worse, I was determined not to let our baby die in hospital. We both wanted him to be able to die at home, but one day, after about a year of his being so ill, he became very sick and started to have fits. He began to struggle for breath. We took him to the doctor who made it clear that we would no longer be able to care for him at home. James and I took the baby to hospital. I knew that I could no longer cope at home, but I still feel so guilty. Our precious baby died soon after.'

My position
I watched Carly relive her most terrible loss. I felt her grieving deeply, and I listened to her describe the prison of her profound guilt. I neither negated her guilt nor confirmed it. I had learnt from Carly just to be there, to go with her. This I did by offering acceptance for her grief. I had tears in my eyes as I felt her pain. We were no longer assuming any client-therapist roles. We are both mothers and I had no hesitation in connecting with her pain and loss.

Five months later
Carly still consulted with me, but on a less frequent basis. She was looking good: more open and more confident. She had, however, stopped exercising because of a knee injury. We both thought that we were nearing the end of therapy. Then Carly made me another collage. The most interesting aspect of this proved to be the strong desire for another child. She had discussed this with James who, after careful consideration, agreed – on one condition. Should the

tests show that the foetus had the same illness suffered by their second baby, Carly would agree to an abortion. She was willing. Then Carly and James attended a group that was being run along the lines of transactional analysis. Here they learned more about their marital relationship, with Carly controlling and James capitulating. Their communication improved. The group facilitator felt that Carly should be more open about expressing her feelings. Being the conscientious person that she is, she opened herself to all of her feelings, including anger, irritation and grief at her loss. She learnt to share these uncensored feelings with her husband, sister and business partner. It seemed that when she was able to share her tears and ask for comfort, she no longer needed anger and irritation. These feelings appeared to result from holding on to great pain. She had previously shown the anger and irritation only to James and her daughter, Melanie. Carly felt vulnerable once she began to express her feelings.

More triggers
Suddenly, Carly's father became critically ill. The doctors felt that he would not live much longer. This impending loss again brought Carly's deep insecurity to the surface. By sharing her feelings during therapy, she decided that she needed to stay strong for her parents and must put her own feelings aside. We talked about her father and his relationship with her mother and with herself. Carly felt terrified of losing him and deep sorrow that she would shortly not have a father. At the same time, she was experiencing a slow period at work which added to her insecurity. Carly was also dealing with a particularly demanding business client at this time. Their relationship had shifted when the client began to confide her personal problems to Carly. This client needed an enormous amount of emotional support. Carly was at a vulnerable stage in her life. She identified with her client's pain and tried to resolve her problems for her. Carly was too heavily burdened and did not have the emotional resources to cope.

The final straw
Carly knew that there was a reasonable chance of her next baby having the same disease. Whilst intellectually she had accepted this risk and the chance of abortion, emotionally she had not been able to do so. She had realised this one day when she had listened

to a speech on abortion. She had sat and sobbed. She was grieving the fact that she would never have another child. As she had come from a family of five children, she had always wanted a large family of her own. One child did not make up a 'family' in her eyes. She said, 'Sue, I'm trying so hard but I'm not coping. I'm totally exhausted. I'm not sleeping and I can't eat at all. I'm so frightened. I'm losing control. I feel like I did when I was depressed.'

Carly's sister phoned me to say that she was extremely concerned and to ask me to make contact with Carly at home. I phoned Carly who asked me to visit her at home. There, I met James and Carly's mother. Carly had withdrawn to a place where no one could reach her. Her eyes were glazed and she hardly moved. She was a little better when I arrived but still profoundly depressed. She spoke to me, but very slowly. She had no appetite and had not eaten any solid food for a week. She had been drinking a liquid supplement. She had been waking up in the morning with terrible feeling of anxiety in the pit of her stomach. Any activity exhausted her, even swallowing her diet supplement.

It was time to refer Carly to the psychiatrist she had seen after her baby's death. She needed antidepressant medication and tranquillisers. Her inability to eat indicated the possibility of hospitalisation. Carly was against the idea of hospitalisation because she felt that being on her own all day would make her feel worse.

Carly's psychiatrist is one of my favourites. He respects his clients and is a true expert in the field of psychotropic medication. He examined Carly the following morning and prescribed Prozac® for the depression and Xanor® for her severe anxiety and restlessness. It took two and a half weeks for the medication to start working.

James

James had told me that whilst Carly was no longer 'scapegoating' him with her anger and irritation, she was still quick to anger. Recently, an egg had fallen on the ground and smashed. She had cursed and slammed doors. When this happened, he and Melanie would shudder from the explosions and tensions, even if they had not been directed at them. The atmosphere at home had been unpredictable. Carly was surprised to hear his view. James was not used to expressing his feelings at home.

I had asked to meet with James in my consulting rooms as I felt that he was carrying many unspoken, but nevertheless strong feelings. Carly also wanted him to meet with me because she felt it would give him a greater understanding of depression and how to cope with it. James had been reluctant to meet with me, but finally had.

Carly had said that her father was like a saint: kind and good to everyone. James and I discussed how she may have married a prototype of her father – James.

James explained to me that he enjoyed caring for people and that he was a caring, nurturing person by nature. He also told me that their transactional analysis group facilitator had described him as a tree that was always bending, but might snap if he leaned any further. James continued, 'Carly tries to control everything. She's insecure about money, so she goes overboard on controlling our spending. On holiday, however, she spends and spends because we are on holiday. This doesn't make sense to me. When I drive she tells me how to drive and where to drive. She has made our home her family's home. Her mother and sister have keys to our home and can come and go at will. I have no privacy. What would happen if one of them walked in while I was walking around naked? She's used to a big family with no boundaries. It's a case of "my home is your home". I hate that! If I'm making supper for Melanie and myself on evenings when she is going to an AA meeting, or doesn't feel like eating, she tells me what to cook. I want to cook what I want to eat. This controlling of Carly's has gone on for as long as I've known her.

'This depression is the third. We haven't had a lot of fun over the past eight years – only small patches. But this time I'm scared. I've never seen Carly so far gone. Despite what I've just said, I love her very much. She is my friend and I don't know how to help her. We've survived so much in our life together, but this time she has withdrawn so far away from me. Must I cajole her out of bed? Must I insist that she eats? What must I do?'

I asked James whether he had expressed his dissatisfactions and needs to Carly. He said that he had, but quietly. She had always told him that he was wrong and that she was right, and so the status quo had remained. I asked why he had never expressed himself more loudly and more often. He said, 'When I've tried to do so, Carly either explodes, swearing and cursing and we end up having a fiery argument, or she withdraws for long periods and sulks and won't talk to me. I hate that and I'm basically a peaceful person who avoids conflict.' I explained to James that he could and should express his needs in an assertive manner. He should also refuse unreasonable requests, based on his 'gut' feel. I told him that he had been 'walking on eggs' for too long. Direct communication was, in fact, what Carly had been asking for from those close to her. She had told me that this would help her to know how people close to her were feeling and what they wanted. Up till then, she had not been listening to James. Also, James had not spoken assertively enough. James reported to Carly that our session had been productive and they discussed his needs.

I also told James not to be Carly's 'caretaker', as this would help to keep her depressed. One way to change this role was to avoid cajoling and encouraging her out of her depression. The pace of her improvement would be guided by her own energy levels. He should invite her to join him and Melanie on outings or activities at home. Then he needed to respect her wish to join them or to remain on her own. I knew that Carly was determined to feel better, but that her improvement would be at her own rate – mainly contingent on her energy levels.

Carly's business partner, Sally
Carly asked me to contact Sally because the latter wanted to know how best to cope. We initially spoke on the telephone, then later with Carly in my rooms. I explained how she could cope with Carly's depression in much the same way as I had with James: don't push or cajole – respect Carly's pace of improvement. At the same time, feel free to express your feelings honestly. Sally was better able to do this than James. She had, for example, told Carly that she was not going to be visiting her at home at the weekend as she did not feel like being part of all the depression. She had also told Carly that she would cope with running their business while Carly recovered. She had chosen to postpone a long-awaited holiday until Carly felt strong enough to run the business again.

Within this business relationship Carly interacted in a diametrically opposite manner to the way she interacted with James. With Sally, Carly was very polite and grateful. It was here that her worst feelings of indebtedness and worthlessness arose.

She felt that she could never show sufficient gratitude for the heavy burdens that she had 'dumped' on Sally over the years. Sally reassured Carly that even though she was pressured by the extra responsibility, it had been her choice to take it on and that there was no possibility of Sally wanting to dissolve their partnership – a huge fear of Carly's.

I watched Carly defining herself as psychologically 'inferior' in relation to Sally's 'superior' position. It showed in her pleasing tone of voice. It showed in her expressions of ever-lasting indebtedness and in her praising of everything that Sally was and everything that she did. I pointed out this observation to Carly in a subsequent session.

Carly's mother and sister
At the start of this depression, Carly had been torn between her strong feelings of dependence on her mother and her sister for emotional support, and her need to be strong and dependable for the family – especially in the light of her father's illness. Carly's conflict was resolved by the increasing severity of her depression. Her mother made herself available to care for Carly – but only at Carly's request. Her sister, like James, was frightened. This was the worst depression that she had ever seen. She, too, wanted to know how to help. Carly seemed to relax in this sub-system, in that she was now easily able to ask for the kind of support that she needed. She did not mix this request for help with irritation or anger.

This is a family who give to each other. I have never met with Carly's brothers, but have heard a fair amount about one brother's strong movement towards religion and away from alcohol. The other brother has been described in terms of his wife's difficulties in coping with his alcohol problem and the family's support of her.

Sharon, the homoeopath
At the deepest stages of Carly's severe depression, her friend, Sharon, a medical doctor now practising homoeopathy, arrived for a visit from New Zealand. She made contact with Carly. They had shared a great friendship when she and Carly were living in Australia. Since Sharon had met Carly socially during her postnatal depression, we all agreed that Sharon should treat her homoeopathically for the grief reaction that she was presenting here. This treatment would assist, initially, with her terrible early-

morning anxiety and later work on her grief. The early-morning agitation lessened considerably after three days. The psychiatrist and I were fully supportive of Sharon's entry into the homoeopathic treatment arena. Carly felt good about her friend's treatment, especially as it was seen as complementary to her psychotropic medication. She continued to take the homoeopathic remedy once a week.

Carly had, by now, learned to feel her grief and to cry when she was sad. Members of her system were aware of the most beneficial role for each to assume. Everyone, including Carly, was talking openly and honestly and respectfully to each other.

Up to the present

Carly's energy improved although it was still limited. She began to experience a 'normal' hour now and then, a 'normal' few hours, then a 'normal' afternoon. Afternoons were usually better for her than mornings. The mornings, however, were no longer as bad they had been. I suggested that she listen to her body in terms of how much she did on a day, and that she stop when she became tired. It seems that when a depressed client pushes past their fatigue, they suffer a relapse. At this time Carly began to exercise again – first for 10 minutes at a time, then building up to 40 minutes per day. She set the limit at 40, although I had said that 20-30 minutes was fine. She was sleeping well and eating small amounts of solid food on a regular basis. She looked much better, a good indication being the clarity of her eyes.

She still had periods of enormous sadness and expressed this with tears and verbalisation of her feelings. She had regular contact with her minister of religion and continued to attend AA meetings twice a week. Her relationships at home were getting better and better. Her anger and irritation had gone. She said, 'I feel as if I've been stripped of every cover I've ever found familiar. I'm like a new-born baby. I have no protective skin. I can no longer behave as I did in the past. I feel very open and vulnerable and really feel things for the first time. Even though it is painful, I know it is right. I feel incredibly close to James. We talk and touch and, believe it or not, we make love. I screamed at James in front of Melanie and her cousins a while ago and he told me never to speak to him in such a denigrating manner again, especially not in front of Melanie. I nearly did what I used to do – curse, swear, argue and sulk for days, but instead I simmered for a bit and then went to him to talk it through. We both apologised and had a lovely day. I rest when I'm tired and I do things when I've got the energy. I'm asking James for hugs. It's funny, I find that when I give him something, even understanding, he gives me back three times as much, its so easy. Something so different happened to us that I can hardly believe it:

We were driving on the highway – I've stopped telling him how to drive – when he shifted into the wrong gear and the engine blew. We pushed the car to the side of the road and both laughed! I previously would have screamed at his stupidity and castigated him for days for costing us so much money. I no longer feel the need to control the uncontrollable. I have managed to look after Melanie and her friends to give James a chance to take a break or have a sleep. I have been going in to work for a short while every day, but I'm totally resistant. This is not to do with depression. I don't know why I have to struggle to overcome my resistance to work.'

This is where Carly and I are at present. We are going to work on her feelings of inferiority and her indebtedness to Sally. She needs to gradually redefine herself as equal to Sally in order to move on. We will continue to face her issues that surface, as and when they do so. This is one courageous woman!

SUMMARY

In this part of the book, I wanted to paint you a minimalistic landscape of theories of and psychotherapeutic approaches to depression. I described the case of Carly and the people close to her to illustrate how I work in therapy with depression – an inclusive systems approach.

PART 5

HOLISTIC APPROACH TO DEPRESSION

There are a number of reasons why this book did not end at Part 4:

- I have felt comfortable and confident in discussing self-help, medical and psychological approaches to depression with you.
- Feeling comfortable and confident has always been a trigger for me to move into less familiar, but nevertheless fascinating areas of knowledge.
- Many of my clients have spoken of their experiences with holistic types of healing for physical and emotional distress and for increasing their general resistance to ill-health. My clients have consulted the experts in the various holistic fields and have, in general, taken responsibility for their own wellbeing. They have utilised a combination of therapies that fit with their lifestyles and are not exorbitantly expensive. The holistic option is thus also beneficial in that it is, in general, available to people irrespective of their income (a major disadvantage of some of the other very expensive therapies such as psychotherapy and psychotropic medication).
- A major eye-opener for me, however, was a visit to the 'Living Art Exhibition' held annually at the University of Cape Town. This was a display of hundreds of holistic therapies including art, movement, homoeopathy, massage, spiritual healing, shaitsu, Reiki, health foods and vitamins, aromatherapy and many others! I have seldom seen so many people so enthusiastic and involved at one event. The people filled a very large area. One could hardly move for the sheer press of bodies. The message to me was that there are healing modalities that have

been in existence for far longer than the medical or psychological therapies and that they are presently in enormous demand.
- It is likely that many of you know more about these approaches than I do. This, in itself, is a reason for extending this book into the holistic area. It will, hopefully, open further channels of communication between you and me, and you and others. This part of the book has been written to whet your appetite for the banquet of ongoing learning and knowledge that exists in the universe.
- Although much of the available literature about holistic therapies focuses on general physical and emotional wellbeing and balance, I have not yet found any works that focus solely on depression. There are sections of books that address this problem, but my aim is to open discussion of some of the holistic therapies and their applications to depression. It is important to understand, however, that holistic treatment will always examine and treat the 'whole' person rather than 'depression' per se.
- If one or more of these remedies works to improve the quality of your life, or if they are used beneficially in a complementary way with one or more of the other approaches to depression, then I have achieved my aim:
- I hope to provide you with the broadest possible repertoire of resources to use for a healthy balanced life and to ease depression. As with the other approaches mentioned in this book, I would encourage you to read further and learn as much as you can and, if possible, find experts in the various fields who will respect your uniqueness, and who will work with you to reveal your own potential for further growth through knowledge.
- The holistic therapies discussed here are just a few of the many that are available. They serve as examples and not as a comprehensive exploration of this vast field of knowledge.

This information is a combination of my reading of some of the available literature and conversations and personal letters to me from:

- a medical doctor who has trained as a homoeopath – she works

in a complementary way with a medical practitioner steeped in the value of psycho-pharmacology, who readily refers grieving patients for spiritual counselling
- a pharmacist who is a practising homoeopath, and trains medical doctors to become homoeopaths
- a pharmacist who is now a full-time aromatherapist who trains students of aromatherapy and has discovered a huge market for her special blends of essential aromatherapy oils for the bath, the oil burner and for massage
- a medical doctor who practises acupuncture
- a practising psychiatrist who is comfortable about the complementary role of homoeopathy, vitamins and minerals alongside his prescriptions of psychotropic medications and psychotherapy

My communications with all these experts confirm my belief that we can all work well, together with you, in an inclusive, complementary way, rather than in an exclusive restrictive manner.

ACUPUNCTURE

WHAT IS ACUPUNCTURE?

Acupuncture forms an important part of traditional Chinese medicine. It involves the insertion of fine needles into points on the body and burning of herbs. The aim of this process is to stimulate these points of the body to heal themselves specifically or to heal the whole body. Acupuncture is an energy medicine that changes the flow or quality of energy. There are three main methods of acupuncture:

- Traditional: This is aimed at the prevention of ill-health, and the maintenance of good health.
- First Aid: This is aimed at the short-term relief of symptomatic discomfort or pain.
- Anaesthetic: This involves the use of acupuncture alone or together with anaesthetics during surgical operations.

HOW DOES ACUPUNCTURE WORK WITH DEPRESSION?

Severe lack of energy (fatigue, lethargy, poor motivation) is a common symptom of depression as are anxiety and agitation.

Acupuncture works to balance the flow of energy, to energise the body and mind and to calm and soothe tension and agitation.

ALEXANDER TECHNIQUE

What is the Alexander Technique?

This is the observation and correction of unnatural posture, movement and balance. The aim of re-educating the client to improve posture, movement and balance is to relax physical and emotional tensions and thereby to promote a less stressed and more fully functioning existence. Here the therapist or teacher shows the client how to rediscover his or her natural, stress-free posture, movement and balance. Through the course of lessons, the client is re-educated to stand, sit, move and balance in a better way.

How does the Alexander Technique work with depression?

It works to improve sleep habits (a primary problem with depression), increases overall cheerfulness and concentration and, as mentioned earlier, it works to reduce stress, a major component of a depressed system.

AROMATHERAPY

Aromatherapy is a natural, non-invasive use of the essential oils that have a soothing and uplifting effect on the body and the mind. These oils may be used for massage by an aromatherapist, self-massage, in the bath or for burning in an aromatherapy oil burner.

What aromatherapy oils or combinations of these oils have antidepressant properties, and for which depressive symptoms?

- *Camomile, lavender, ylang ylang and sandlewood:* These are sedative oils that are used when the depressed client presents with symptoms of restlessness and disturbed sleep patterns.
- *Bergamot, geranium and grapefruit:* These are uplifting oils, used when the depressed client is fatigued and lethargic.
- *Bergamot:* This oil is soothing and is used for depressed clients who present with chronic anxiety, frustration and suppressed anger.

- *Sweet orange and mandarin:* These are also soothing oils and are used for the depressed client who is experiencing severe anxiety and negative thought patterns.
- *Camomile:* This calming oil is used for the depressed client who is moody and irritable.
- *Rose, jasmine and neroli:* These oils are comforting and nourish the soul. They are used when a depressed client is suffering from severe anxiety.
- *Jasmine:* This is an oil that is uplifting, builds confidence and re-establishes warmth for the depressed client who is low in confidence, inhibited, who represses feelings, is vulnerable but feels emotionally cold.
- *Rose:* This oil stabilises emotions and is used for depressed clients who experience severe mood swings.
- *Neroli:* This is a spiritually uplifting oil that is used to alleviate the despair and despondency of depression.
- *Rosemary:* This is a stimulant that works on the apathy and mental fatigue often presented in depressed clients.
- *Frankincense and Vetivier:* These oils promote tranquillity in depressed clients who tend to be obsessive worriers.

My clients who are depressed, as well as those close to them, speak highly of the beneficial effects of aromatherapy, especially for calming their tensions. They talk of 'melting' out of the aromatherapist's rooms and especially enjoying the touch connection.

I also regularly use aromatherapy bath oils – some for calming and others for uplifting, depending on my needs at the time. One way of 'balancing' myself – in a most luxurious and pampering way – at the end of a hectic day is to light aromatherapy oils (lavender and geranium) in a burner, with candlelight and soft music and I think I go to Heaven! It feels as if every sense is being stimulated, creating a wonderfully pampered sense of wellbeing.

HOMOEOPATHY

What is homoeopathy?

Homoeopathy is a mode of treatment that aims at understanding the whole person in terms of physical and emotional functioning.

The homoeopath examines the client's physical and emotional lifestyle when the client is feeling well and when he or she is manifesting ill-health. 'Well' is defined as 'balanced', while 'ill' or 'sick' is seen as 'out of balance'. This treatment, like many holistic therapies, works on maximising energy balance. This form of therapy is used both for immediate, short-term relief of acute symptoms and for more long-term, general wellbeing.

The homoeopath forms a 'symptom picture' of all the client's conditions, symptoms and lifestyle preferences and attempts to fit or match the symptom picture to a symptom picture of homoeopathic remedy. The remedy chosen emphasises this symptom picture and artificially mirrors it, thereby bringing it to the surface. This process seems to activate the client's own self-healing mechanisms so that natural healing can occur.

How does homoeopathy define depression?

This form of therapy views depression as an expression of an imbalance of energy, where the client is out-of-tune with his or her life source. The homoeopath does not lay too much emphasis on understanding the symptoms of depression, but rather on the way in which the depressed client expresses his or her despair and despondancy.

What remedies exist for the treatment of depression?

Many homoeopathic remedies are available for this purpose. The choice of which to use depends on the remedy that best matches the symptom picture presented by the client. The skilled homoeopath will use one or more remedies in sequence as the individual symptom picture emerges and/or changes. These remedies include:

- *Argentum Nitricum* for restless, apprehensive and agitated depression, often accompanied by anticipatory anxiety.
- *Arsenicum Album* for agitated depression, often accompanied by physical symptoms affecting the stomach, such as diarrhoea.
- *Aurum Metallicum* (the most commonly used remedy for depression) for the depressed person who blames him or herself for everything and feels worthless.

- *Ignatia Amara* for a depression where the client is unable to control his or her feelings. There is often a combination of laughter and tears, or periods of severe withdrawal and others of loud distress. This remedy is frequently used where the aetiology is grief.
- *Lachesis* for a depression characterised by withdrawal, paranoia and distrust, where the client is normally outgoing and trusting.
- *Natrium Muriaticum* for a well-concealed depression that the client rationalises as his or her lot in life, or as part of general human existence. Grief or loss is usually paramount in this remedy picture.
- *Nux Vomica* for a depression characterised by anger and irritation together with exhaustion from overwork.
- *Pulsatilla Nigricans* for depression with strong elements of dependency on others with self-pity, weepiness and fears of rejection.
- *Sepia* for depression where the client is totally withdrawn, with occasional outbursts of anger. The client displays general irritability, a critical attitude towards others and negativity.
- *Staphysagria* for depression characterised by the client suppressing his or her feelings. This remedy picture is characterised by the client's strong sense of feeling abused with passive-aggressive features.

Please do not self-medicate with homoeopathic remedies as some of these could have adverse side-effects when taken in incorrect doses or for the wrong reasons. The skilled homoeopath will stop, change or combine different remedies as the client's symptom picture alters through the course of therapy.

An interesting example of the use of homoeopathy in dealing with depression is the story of Carly. There we find the combined use of psychotherapy, psychotropic medication (Prozac®, Eglonyl® and Xanor®), vitamins and minerals (Dolomite® with calcium, vitamin D and magnesium) together with the homoeopathic remedy – *Nux Vomica*. Her homoeopath told Carly that after a three- day course of this remedy, the terrible agitation that she experienced in the morning would be much better. This happened. Further she was told that a subsequent weekly dose of the same remedy would be followed by the release of her grief. This, too, happened.

REFLEXOLOGY

WHAT IS REFLEXOLOGY?

This is a form of massage where the reflexologist works with his or her thumbs, and sometimes fingers, on reflex areas on the feet and sometimes on the hands. These reflex areas relate to specific parts of the body.

In general, the reflexologist works on the feet because these are more responsive than the hands.

Reflexology is used both as treatment for ill-health and, as with other holistic therapies, as a prevention of illness and for the maintenance of good health and wellbeing.

The whole surface of both feet or both hands is treated. This brings the entire body into balance. When certain areas of physical or emotional function are presenting as problems, they are given special attention.

HOW IS REFLEXOLOGY USED IN THE TREATMENT OF DEPRESSION?

The reflexologist describes depression as a lowering of the physical and mental state of the body. This form of treatment improves the physical wellbeing of the body and thus raises the mental state of the client.

There are certain reflex areas that are most pertinent to the direct treatment of depression. These are called the 'DRs of depression' and are found in the thumbs and big toes. The reflexologist will also work on reflex areas that are associated with depression. These are called the 'ARs of depression' and are found on the:

- big toes and thumbs which relate to the head, pituitary and brain
- the pad just below the big toes and on the thumbs which relate to the thyroid gland
- the soft inner arch of each foot and the palm of the hands between the thumb and the index fingers which relate to the adrenal glands
- just below the pad under the toes and high on the palm of the hand, about midway between the thumb and index finger which they relate to the solar plexus

- on the outer foot, below the ankle bone, and at the base of the pad under the thumb which relate to the reproductive organs

Summary

In this part of the book I have attempted to extend the healing of depression into the field of holistic therapies. Examples of these have been discussed. It seems that these forms of therapy use different means to access the client's life source (energy) and to move towards a physical and emotional sense of balance.

While my focus has been on the depressed client, these therapies are also worth considering for the balance and wellbeing of those who are close to someone who is depressed.

CONCLUDING COMMENTS

I began this book because I felt a strong need to translate academic research and subsequent experience into user-friendly and accessible material. As happens with books, however, it has taken on a life of its own and moved with me into unexpected nooks and crannies and broad unchartered seas of experience. It has been like an unplanned adventure where some doors were firmly shut in my face, but other unexpected ones opened in front of me. I have felt challenged and exhilarated, saddened and exhausted. I do not remember experiencing so many diverse feelings flowing through me and out of my pen ever before.

    I had hoped to write a positive book on depression. Positive does not, however, mean without pain or tears. Life energies ebb and flow as the waves of the sea and as day and night. I hope that you will open yourself and connect with your own unique flow, that you will feel high on the joys and excitements and flow into the dark for rest and replenishment. Know that the lows are as transient – but as important – as the highs. Maximise each phase of your wave and know that there is help outside should you feel debilitated in the dark or out of control. And above all, remember – be kind to yourself.

FOOTNOTES

PART 1
1 Barchas, J.D., Patrick, R.L., Raese, J. and Berger, P.A. (1977). Neuropharmacological aspects of affective disorders. In J. Usdin (Ed.), *Depression. Clinical, biological and psychological perspectives.* New York. Brunner/Mazel.
Shildkrant, J. (1965). The catecholamine hypothesis of affective disorders: A review of supporting evidence. *American Journal of Psychiatry,* 123, 201-207.
2 Bunney, W.E. and Fawcett, J.A. (1965). Possibility of a biochemical test for suicidal potential: an analysis of endocrine findings prior to three suicides. *Archives of General Psychiatry,* 13, 232-239.
3 Gibbons, J.L. (1960). Total body sodium and potassium in depressive illness. *Clinical Sciences,* 19, 133-138.
4 Mackay, D. (1975). *Clinical psychology: theory and therapy.* Methuen.

PART 2
1 Noakes, T. (1992). *Lore of running.* Oxford University Press.
2 Carter, R. (1977). Exercise and happiness. *Journal of Sports Medicine,* 17, 307-313.
3 Nouri, S. and Beer, J. (1989). Relations of moderate physical exercise to scores on hostility, aggression, and trait-anxiety. *Perceptive and Motor Skills,* 68, 1191-1194.
4 Stephens, T. (1988). Physical activity and mental health in the United States and Canada: Evidence from four population surveys. *Preventive Medicine,* 17, 35-47.
5 Smith, M. (1975). *When I say no I feel guilty.* Bantam Books.
6 Peck, S. (1978). *The road less travelled.* Arrow Books.

PART 3
1. Barchas, J.D., Patrick, R.L., Raese, J., and Berger, P.A. (1977). Neuropharmacological aspects of affective disorders. In J. Usdin (Ed.), *Depression. Clinical, biological and psychological perspectives.* New York.
2. Bunney, W.E. and Fawcett, J.A. (1965). Possibility of a biochemical test for suicidal potential: an analysis of endocrine findings prior to three suicides. *Archives of General Psychiatry, 13,* 232-239.
   Gibbons, J.L. (1960). Total body sodium and potassium in depressive illness. *Clinical Sciences, 19,* 133-138.
3. Winkour, G. (1981). *Depression. The facts.* Oxford University Press.
4. Talmud, J. (1993). Pharmacological management of depression. *Modern Medicine of South Africa,* 116-117.

PART 4
1. Abrahams, M.J. and Whitlock, F.A. (1969). Childhood experience and depression. *British Journal of Psychiatry, 115,* 883-888.
2. Isenberg, P.L. and Shatzberg, A.F. (1978). Psychoanalytic contribution to a theory of depression. In J.O. Cole, A.F. Shatzberg & S.H. Frazier (Eds.), *Depression, biology, psychodynamics and treatment.* Plenum Press.
   White, R.B. (1977). Current psychoanalytic concepts of depression. In W.E. Fann, I. Karacan, A.D. Pokorny & R.L. Williams (Eds.), *Phenomenology and treatment of depression.* Spectrum.
3. Freud, S. (1962). Mourning and melancholia (1917). In S. Freud (Ed.), *The standard edition of the complete psychological works of Sigmund Freud.* (Vol 14)., 311-333. Hogarth Press and the Institute of Psychoanalysis.
4. Mendelson, M. (1974). *Psychoanalytic concepts of depression.* Spectrum.
5. Cohen, M.B., Baker, G., Cohen R.A., Fromm-Reichmann, F., and Weigert, E.V. (1954). An intensive study of twelve cases of manic-depressive psychosis. *Psychiatry, 17,* 103-137.
6. Ferster, C.B. (1974). Behavioral approaches to depression. In R.J. Friedman and M.M. Katz (Eds.), *The psychology of depression: contemporary theory research.* Wiley.
7. Mclean, P.D. (1981). Behavioral treatment of depression. In W.D. Craighead, A.E. Kazdin and M.J. Mahoney (Eds.), *Behavior modification. Principles, issues and applications.* Houghton-Mifflin Co.
8. Seligman, M.E.P. (1974). Depression and learned helplessness. In R.J. Friedman & M.M. Katz (Eds.), *The psychology of depression:*

contemporary theory and research. Wiley.

Seligman, M.E.P. (1975). *Helplessness. On depression, development and death.* W.H. Freeman.

9   Lazarus, A.A. (1974). Multi-modal behavioral treatment of depression. *Behavior Therapy, 5,* 549-554.

Lewinsohn, P.M. and Shaffer, M. (1971). Use of home observations as an integral part of the treatment of depression. *Journal of Consulting and Clinical Psychology, 37* (1), 87-94.

Smith, M. (1975). *When I say no I feel guilty.* Bantam Books.

10 Liberman, R.P. and Raskin, D.E. (1971). Depression. A behavioural formulation. *Archives of General Psychiatry, 24 (6),* 515-523.

11 Beck, A.T. (1967). *Depression.* Harper & Row.

Beck, A.T. (1974). The development of depression. In R.J. Friedman and M.M. Katz (Eds.), *The psychology of depression: contemporary theory and research.* Wiley.

Beck, A.T. (1976). *Cognitive therapy and emotional disorders.* International Universities Press.

12 Burns, D. (1980). *Feeling good: The new mood therapy.* Signet.

Burns, D. (1989). *The feeling good handbook.* Plume.

13 Kiesler, D.J. (1979). An interpersonal communication analysis of relationships in psychotherapy. *Psychiatry, 42,* 299-311.

14 Berkowitz, D.A. (1981). On the reclaiming of denied affects in family therapy. In J. Berenson & H. White (Eds.), *Annual Review of Family Therapy.* (Vol 1). Human Sciences Press.

15 Rubenstein, D. and Timmins, J.F. (1981). Depressive dyadic and triadic relationships. In J. Berenson and H. White (Eds.), *Annual Review of Family Therapy* (Vol 1). Human Sciences Press.

16 Feldman, L.B. (1981). Depression and marital interaction. In J. Berenson & H. White (Eds.), *Annual Review of Family Therapy.* (Vol 1). Human Sciences Press.

17 Dell, P. (1982). Beyond homeostasis: towards a concept of coherence. *Family Process, 21,* 21-41.

Hoffmann, L. (1981). *Foundations of family therapy.* Basic Books.

Elkaim, M. (1981). Non-equilibrium, chance, and change in family therapy. *Marital and Family Therapy* (Special July Issue).

Keeney, B.P. (1979). Ecosystemic epistemology: an alternative paradigm for diagnosis. *Family Process, 18,* (2), 117-129.

Sluzki, C.E. (1979). Marital therapy from a systems perspective. In T. Paolino & B. McCrady (Eds.), *Marriage and marital therapy.* Brunner/Mazel.

18 Berkowitz, D.A. (1981). On the reclaiming of denied affects in family therapy. In J. Berenson and H. White (Eds.), *Annual Review of Family Therapy*. (Vol 1). Human Sciences Press.
19 Rubenstein, D. and Timmins, J.F. (1981). Depressive dyadic and triadic relationships. In J. Berenson and H. White (Eds.), *Annual Review of Family Therapy*. (Vol 1). Human Sciences Press.
20 Musikanth, S.J. (1981). *Two methods in the treatment of depression*. Unpublished Master's Thesis. University of South Africa.
Musikanth, S. J. (1985). *Client-centred psychotherapy in the treatment of depression - a system's view*. Unpublished Doctoral Thesis. University of South Africa.

RECOMMENDED READING

Abrahams, M.J., and Whitlock, F.A. (1969). Childhood experience and depression. *British Journal of Psychiatry, 115,* 883-888.
Alexander, F.M. (1986). *The use of self.* Centerline.
Barchas, J.D., Patrick, R.L. Raese, J. and Berger, P.A. (1977). Neuropharmacological aspects of affective disorders. In J. Usdin (Ed.), *Depression. Clinical, biological and psychological perspectives.* New York. Brunner/Mazel.
Barlow, W., (1990). *The Alexander technique.* Gollanzc.
Beck, A. (1976). *Cognitive therapy and emotional disorders.* International Universities Press.
Beck, A.T., Ward, C.H., Mendelson, M., Mock, J., and Erbagh, J. (1961). An inventory for measuring depression. *Archives of General Psychiatry, 4,* 561-571.
Berkowitz, D.A. (1981). On the reclaiming of denied affects in family therapy. In J. Berenson and H. White (Eds.). *Annual Review of Family Therapy.* (Vol. 1). Human Sciences Press.
Bunney, W.E., and Fawcett, J.A. (1965). Possibility of a biochemical test for suicidal potential: an analysis of endocrine findings prior to three suicides. *Archives of General Psychiatry, 13,* 232-239.
Burang, T. (1975). *Tibetan art of healing.* Watkins
Burkett, L. (1992). *Victory over debt.* Northfield.
Burns, D. (1980). *Feeling good: The new mood therapy.* Signet.
Burns, D. (1989). *The feeling good handbook.* Plume.
Carnegie, D. (1984). *How to stop worrying and start living.* Revised Edition. Pocket Books.
Carter, R. (1977). Exercise and happiness. *Journal of Sports Medicine, 17,* 307-313.

Cohen, M.B., Baker, G., Cohen, R.A., Fromm-Reichmann, F., and Weigert, E.V. (1954). An Intensive study of twelve cases of manic-depressive psychosis. *Psychiatry, 17,* 103-137.
Copeland, M.E (1994). *Living without depression and manic depression.* New Harbinger Publications.
Davis, P. (1988) *Aromatherapy. An A-Z.* C.W. Daniel Company.
Feldman, L.B. (1981). Depression and marital interaction. In J. Berenson and H. White (Eds.), *Annual Review of Family Therapy.* (Vol. 1). Human Sciences Press
Ferster, C.B. (1974). Behavioral approaches to depression. In R.J. Friedman and M.M. Katz (Eds.), *The psychology of depression: contemporary theory research.* Wiley.
Freud, S. (1962). Mourning and Melancholia (1917). In S. Freud (Ed.), *The standard edition of the complete psychological works of Sigmund Freud.* (Vol. 14). 311-333. Hogarth Press and the Institute of Psychoanalysis.
Gibbons, J.L. (1960). Total body sodium and potassium in depressive illness. *Clinical Sciences, 19,* 133-138.
Gorman, J. (1991). *The essential guide to psychotropic medications.* St. Martin's Press.
Haas, E.M. (1981). *Staying healthy with the seasons.* Celestial Arts.
Hall, M. (1991). *Reflexology – A way to better health.* Gateway Books.
Handley, R. (1995). *Homoeopathy for emotional health.* Thorsons.
Hayley, J. (1963). *Strategies of psychotherapy.* Grune & Stratton.
Hodgkinson, L. (1988). *The Alexander technique and how it can help you.* Piatkus Books
Isenberg, P.L., and Schatzberg, A.F. (1978). Psychoanalytic contribution to a theory of depression. In J.O. Cole, A.F. Shatzberg and S.H. Frazier (Eds.), *Depression, biology, psychodynamics and treatment.* Plenum Press.
Jacobson, E. (1968). *Progressive relaxation.* University of Chicago Press.
Kaptchuk, T.J. (1987). *Chinese medicine: The web that has no weaver.* Century Publishing.
Kehoe, J. (1991). *Money success and you.* Zoetic Inc.
Kiesler, D.J. (1979). An interpersonal communication analysis of relationships in psychotherapy. *Psychiatry, 42,* 299-311.
Lee, N.C. (1992). Pharmacological management of depression. *CME, 10,* 295-298.
Lewinsohn, P., Munoz, R., Youngren, M.A. and Zeiss, A. (1986).

Control your depression. Prentice-Hall.
Liberman, R.P. and Raskin, D.E. (1971). Depression. A behavioral formulation. *Archives of General Psychiatry, 24(6),* 515-523.
Looker, T.S, and Gregson, O. (1989). *Stresswise.* Hodder & Stroughton.
Mackay, D. (1975) *Clinical psychology: theory and therapy.* Methuen.
May, R. (1980). *The courage to create.* Bantam Books.
Mclean, P.D. (1981). Behavioral treatment of depression. In W.D. Craighead, A.E. Kazdin and M.J. Mahoney (Eds.), *Behavior modification. Principles, issues and applications.* Houghton-Mifflin Co.
Mendelson, M. (1974). *Psychoanalytic concepts of depression.* Spectrum.
Mindell, E. (1985). *The vitamin bible.* Arlington Books.
Musikanth, S.J. (1981). *Two methods in the treatment of depression.* Unpublished Master's Thesis, University of South Africa.
Musikanth, S.J. (1985). *Client-centred psychotherapy in the treatment of depression – a system's view.* Unpublished Doctoral Thesis. University of South Africa.
Musikanth, S. (1996). *Stress Matters.* William Waterman.
Musikanth, S.J. and Fourie, D.P. (1983). Depression: a broader perspective. *South African Journal of Psychology, 13(4),* 119-127.
Noakes, T. (1992). *Lore of Running.* Oxford University Press.
Nouri, S. and Beer, J. (1989). Relations of moderate physical exercise to scores on hostility, aggression, and trait-anxiety. *Perceptive and Motor Skills, 68,* 1191-1194.
Olsen, K. (1989). *The encyclopaedia of alternative health care.* Piatkus
Olsen, K. (1992). *The encyclopaedia of alternative health care.* Piatkus
Peck, S. (1978). *The road less travelled.* Arrow Books.
Rubenstein, D. and Timmins, J.F. (1981). Depressive dyadic and triadic relationships. In J. Berenson and H. White (Eds.), *Annual Review of Family Therapy.* (Vol.1). Human Sciences Press.
Shein, J., and Hansten, P. (1993) *The consumer's guide to drug interactions.* Collier Books.
Smith, M. (1975). *When I say no, I feel guilty.* Bantam Books.
Smith, T. (1987). *Understanding homoeopathy.* Insight Editions.
Stephens, T. (1988). Physical activity and mental health in the United States and Canada: Evidence from four population surveys. *Preventive Medicine, 17,* 35-47.
Talmud, J. (1993). Pharmacological management of depression. *Modern Medicine of South Africa,* 116-117.

Ullman, D. (1989). *Homoeopathy: Medicine for the 21st century.* Thorsons.
Vithoulkas, G. (1986). *The science of homoeopathy.* Thorsons.
Westfieldt, L. (1984). *F. Matthias Alexander: The man and his work.* Centerline Press.
White, R.B. (1977). Current psychoanalytic concepts of depression. In W.E. Fann, I. Karacan, A.D. Pokorny, and R.L. Williams (Eds.), *Phenomenology and treatment of depression.* Spectrum.
Whittaker, N. and Heystek, M. (1990). *Making money made simple.* Struik Timmins.
Winkour, G. (1981). *Depression. The facts.* Oxford University Press.

ORDER FORM

I wish to purchase .... relaxation cassettes @ R60.00 each

Total R ....

Name ....

Address ....

.... Postal code ....

Company .... Position ....

Telephone................................... Fax ....

Please tick appropriate box

Enclosed is my cheque ☐ postal order ☐ money order ☐

Cheques, postal orders or money orders to be made out to Matters Inc.

Charge my Visa card ☐ Master card ☐ Expiry date ....

Card no. ☐☐☐☐☐☐☐☐☐☐☐☐☐☐☐☐

Signature ....

Please send this order form together with your payment to:

Matters Inc.
18 Corsair Crescent
Constantia 7800
Cape Town